A Land Fit for Heroin?

Drug policies, prevention and practice

Edited by
Nicholas Dorn
and
Nigel South

M
MACMILLAN
EDUCATION

First published 1987

Published by
MACMILLAN EDUCATION LTD
Houndmills, Basingstoke, Hampshire RG21 2XS
and London
Companies and representatives
throughout the world

Typeset by Wessex Typesetters
(Division of The Eastern Press Ltd)
Frome, Somerset

Printed in Great Britain by
Anchor Brendon Ltd,
Tiptree, Essex

British Library Cataloguing in Publication Data
A land fit for heroin?: drug policies,
prevention and practice.
1. Heroin habit—Great Britain
I. Dorn, Nicholas   II. South, Nigel
362.2′93′0941   HV5822.H4
ISBN 0–333–44151–6 (hardcover)
ISBN 0–333–44152–4 (paperback)

To John Auld

Friend and colleague, who suggested the title and whose companionship, creativity and critical comment we greatly miss

Contents

Acknowledgements

We thank our colleagues at the Institute for the Study of Drug Dependence, in particular Jasper Woodcock for his helpful suggestions. The authors of Chapter 4 add thanks to the Department of Health and Social Security and to a charitable trust for funding two studies drawn upon, and further thanks to Lorraine Lucas and Valerie MacNeshie for transcribing endless taped interviews and drafts.

Nicholas Dorn
Nigel South

Notes on the contributors

Martin Donoghoe is a student in the Department of Applied Social Studies in the Polytechnic of North London.

Nicholas Dorn, PhD, is Assistant Director (Research) at the Institute for the Study of Drug Dependence (ISDD), London. He is author of *Alcohol, Youth and the State* and of several works with Nigel South and others and is a consultant for the United Nations Development Programme.

Betsy Ettorre, PhD, is a Research Associate in the Department of Politics and Sociology at Birkbeck College, University of London. She is author of *Lesbians, Women and Society* and has conducted studies at the Addiction Research Unit, Institute of Psychiatry, London University.

Christine James is a Research Officer at ISDD where she is working on community responses and youth-work practice in relation to drugs. Previously she worked in community work and has studied sociology and health education.

Stephen Jones is a student in the Department of Applied Social Studies in the Polytechnic of North London. During 1986 he and Martin Donoghoe were placement students at ISDD.

Susanne MacGregor, PhD, is Senior Lecturer in the Department of Politics and Sociology at Birkbeck College. She is author of *Politics and Poverty* and a co-author of *Dealing with Drug Misuse* and is directing a major study of the government's Central Funding Initiative on services for drug users.

Geoffrey Pearson is Professor of Social Work at Middlesex Polytechnic. He is author of *The Deviant Imagination* and *Hooligan: A History of Respectable Fears* and recently conducted a study of heroin in the north of England.

Jane Ribbens is a postgraduate student in the Department of Sociology at Essex University. She was formerly a Research Officer at ISDD and co-author of a short book, *Coping with a Nightmare: Family feelings about long term drug use.*

Gerry Stimson, PhD, is Principal Lecturer in Sociology at Goldsmiths College, University of London. He is author of numerous publications on drug problems including *Heroin and Behaviour* and (with Edna Oppenheimer) *Heroin Addiction; Treatment and Control in Britain*.

Nigel South, PhD, is a Research Officer at ISDD. He is co-author with Nicholas Dorn of *Message in a Bottle* and of *Helping Drug Users* and is author of *Policing for Profit: Private Security in Britain*.

List of abbreviations

ACDD	Advisory Committee on Drug Dependence
ACMD	Advisory Council on Misuse of Drugs
ADFAM	Aid for Addicts and Families
CFI	Central Funding Initiative
DAWN	Drugs Alcohol Women Nationally
DDU	Drug Dependency Unit
DHSS	Department of Health and Social Security
ED	Enumeration District (census)
FA	Families Anonymous
GP	General Practitioner (family doctor)
HMSO	Her Majesty's Stationery Office
ISDD	Institute for the Study of Drug Dependence
NACRO	National Association for the Care and Resettlement of Offenders
NIDA	National Institute on Drug Abuse (USA)
OPUS	Organisation of Parents under Stress
PNCB	Pakistan Narcotics Control Board
RCMP	Royal Canadian Mounted Police
RCS	Regional Crime Squad
SCPS	Society of Civil and Public Servants (UK)
UNFDAC	United Nations Fund for Drug Abuse Control

Introduction

Heroin problems have been hitting the headlines recently, in the USA, in Europe and elsewhere. In the USA, heroin remains a serious problem, albeit less 'newsy' than cocaine. Although trends in the extent of use of heroin and related problems seem quite volatile, declining in some parts of that country whilst rising in others, a consistent trend in the mid-1980s has been the availability of heroin of higher purity (NIDA, 1985). In Britain and other European countries, there is no doubt that heroin has become widely available in many regions and neighbourhoods in reasonably high purity (see Chapter 1) and that it is the main drug of public concern – however minor its contribution to mortality and morbidity compared with the records of alcohol and tobacco. In the Third World, Pakistan – the country generally credited with supplying much of the heroin used in Europe in the 1980s – is itself caught up in an escalating cycle of heroin distribution and consumption; similar problems are to be found in several other Asian countries.

In other words, there is a problem – and it is international in scope. In this respect, we have to agree with statements made by a number of governments throughout the 1980s. Although statements about the need for 'a war on drugs' at home and abroad may be making up in excitability for a deficit of effective control measures, it would be wrong to suggest that governments are fighting phantoms. Anybody trading places with a doctor or social worker, with a parent or other relative of someone heavily involved with heroin, with a heroin user him or herself, with a drug trafficker or law enforcement agent would be hard put to maintain that their concerns were purely fictional. The issue is

1

not whether or not there is a problem but what sort of problem it is and, hence, how it is best tackled.

This realisation requires of us that we give up certain habits of thought to which we may still cling. During the 1960s and 1970s it was fashionable in social science and liberal circles to question whether the prevailing concern about drugs use might not be an example of what was termed a 'moral panic' (cf. Cohen, 1980). This term and the paradigm that supported it have now fallen into relative disuse or have been considerably re-cast (Ives, 1986). Nowadays, social scientists have turned from *pronouncing* that popular ideas are examples of 'mystification' or 'false consciousness' and have begun to *ask* how and why popular or leading ideas (e.g. about drugs) win acceptance.

One possible – and perhaps obvious – answer is that modes of thought become popular because they make sense of the social position in which social groups find themselves. This is so in relation to heroin in two senses. First, there really has been a significant increase in the availability of heroin in Britain, and young adults in particular are experimenting with its use in ways that can cause a variety of objective problems. Some of these problems are discussed in this book. Secondly, and less directly but no less powerfully, the spectre of heroin hits a political nerve in Anglo-American cultures – self-indulgence, unbridled pleasuring of self, abuse of the body, the ultimate in empowerment within a private world alongside disempowerment within society. It is noticeable that, when viewed historically, concern over the misuse of heroin and other drugs has only relatively recently arisen in relation to the mature, white, male adult in Western societies. In Britain, from the nineteenth century onwards, the spotlight of concerned reaction has moved from middle class women who used opiates for 'selfish pleasure', to working class female child-minders who dosed their charges to keep them more mangageable (Berridge and Edwards, 1981). In the United States, the focus of concern originally centred upon a range of ethnic minorities (Helmer, 1975) and remained so well into the 1970s. In the post-War period in most 'developed' countries the spotlight fell upon young people. There does seem to be some common thread running through this history. Drug abuse generally, and heroin use specifically, signifies the very *opposite* of the idealised stereotype of masculinity. Drug users are often seen – and, indeed, may sometimes celebrate an identity – as weak, vulnerable, lying, cheating, concerned with pleasure, turning away from responsibility in the world. There is more here than can be captured by the term 'moral panic'.

Given the historical construction of the imagery surrounding heroin, and some contemporary experience of the practice of its widespread use, it is not surprising that public concern runs deep. Although, like others, this social problem is socially and historically constructed, it is sufficiently entrenched to resist being blown away by a few puffs of sociological rhetoric or 'deconstructive' analysis. Heroin problems are as real as, let us say, economic recession. One can no more get rid of them by attempting to define them out of existence than one can get rid of unemployment by such means (although this strategy has indeed been attempted in Britain). However, this is not to say that the problem cannot be mitigated if correctly understood.

How then can we understand the problem of heroin in the late 1980s? At this point we shall attempt to orientate the reader to a framework within which the various authors' contributions to this volume can be placed. Broadly speaking, we can identify three levels of the problem. The first level is primarily economic: the restructuring of the international economy within which, of course, the world trade in drugs takes place. The second level focuses upon the material circumstances and social responses of social groups who may deal in or consume drugs within Western countries (for example, unemployed young white males who come into contact with the drug-distribution system). How people use a drug depends not only on the properties of that drug but also on the cultural resources and needs that they bring to the context in which they use it, and these can be understood in terms of users' social positions. Lastly, there are caring and controlling responses by a range of individuals and institutions – parents (particularly mothers, as we describe) and other relatives, friends of drug users, neighbours and others in local communities, professionals in statutory and non-statutory health and welfare services as well as law enforcement officers.

So far this framework remains very schematic. Selected aspects will be filled out in the following chapters. Let us first however, continue with our overview, which can be represented diagrammatically as shown in Figure I.1.

4

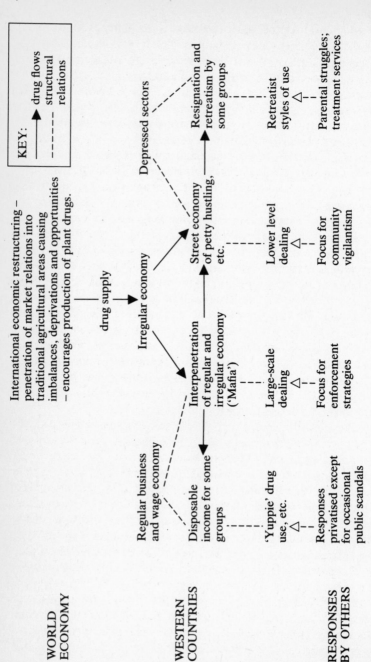

Figure I.1 *Mapping the problem at three levels*

First and most obvious, there has to be some quite substantial level of production of a drug before international trafficking, domestic distribution and individual consumption of it can take place in a widespread manner. In the case of heroin, the essential element in production is cultivation of the opium poppy and harvesting of the milk from its seed pods, for which the chief requirements are hot sun and cheap labour. Since the late 1970s, there has been an increase in cultivation of poppy and production of opium for the manufacture and export of heroin in the Third World – although there have also been shifts in the balance of production between countries. In Chapter 2, Gerry Stimson describes the geo-economic background to this, showing how Third World production of opium fits into the economic and political position of these countries *vis-à-vis* the international order. A colonial history of cash-cropping for export to the more developed countries, the current debt crisis, and the adverse balance of trade provide the conditions in which heroin production is an attractive option for many Third World communities who lack other means of subsistence and advance. The chapter goes on to describe ways in which heroin is imported into developed countries, including Britain, and the prospects for law enforcement at these levels are discussed. Stimson concludes that only genuinely bilateral agreements – recognising the interests of producer and recipient countries – have any prospect of reversing the current trend in international drug supply.

The next 'level' in our general framework for understanding the problem (Figure I.1) is that of the position of social groups in Britain and other Western countries in relation to recent developments in the economy. At this intermediate level (between large-scale supply and individual consumers) the activities of those in the drug-distribution business are of great importance. Recently, popular and academic attention has been drawn to the hidden, unofficial, 'grey' or informal economy, and to the extent to which this may expand in times of recession and restructuring of the formal or regular economy. Many aspects of this informal economy are of no consequence for the drug problem; for example, doing odd jobs 'off the books' or neighbourly reciprocation of goods and services in kind rather than in cash. Other aspects such as home-brewing or wine-making for household consumption or local sale are of potential interest, increasing amounts of alcohol being produced in this way, at low cost and duty-free. The part of the informal economy that is of greatest interest from the point of view of concern with drugs use and availability is its 'irregular' part. This encompasses more overtly criminal activities such as theft, 'fencing' stolen goods, dealing in illegal services, etc. The distribution system for heroin and other drugs inhabits the broader, vigorous irregular economy. This should not however be considered as something entirely separate from the regular economy, as many studies have described the link between the two: the irregular economy (and drug dealing) is simply a high-risk, high-return extension of the regular or formal economy. Persons bridging these sectors (for example, historically, the Mafia) are the mainstay of higher-level drug distribution. They are the focus for law enforcement strategies, such as the increase in the maximum penalty for supply of drugs to life imprisonment and confiscation of assets resulting from crime. Judging from past decades' experience however, increases in penalties alone cannot deter drug distribution – rather, such increases appear to force out relative amateurs and to 'harden' the trade.

Turning now to lower-level distributors, who may also be quite likely to be users of the drugs in which they deal, we can situate this type between the irregular economy and a third sector – the depressed sector of the economy (see Figure I.1). User-dealers with limited licit sources of finance operate in an opportunistic style within the local street economy, interspersing petty theft, burglary, dealing in drugs and generally providing services at the edge of and beyond the law. A key aspect of this role is the highly active, yet erratic pattern of economic and social life (Johnson *et al.*, 1985); drug use occurs here within a context of a life-style of survival on one's wits. Such individuals make a contribution to the recorded rate of property crime, but it is by no means clear that property crimes are *caused* by involvement with drugs: rather, both may be part of the broader pattern of 'making out' (see Chapters 1 and 3).

Next – and in terms of the world literature, most familiarly – we come to the depressed and marginalised classes of society. By this we mean those who at best have only a modest pool of material resources on which to draw and who have been hardest hit by the recession. In most countries, including the UK (and particularly in the north, and parts of London), there are severe pockets of deprivation in which poor housing and industrial collapse coexist. In such contexts young people have little prospects of employment, every prospect of lifelong poverty and no alternatives – except, perhaps, to hustle in the irregular economy, which does not fit the cultural orientations of everyone. If heroin becomes available in such areas then, as Pearson describes in Chapter 3, it is likely to be spread by the hustlers and irregulars to the wider set of young people sharing the experience of economic and social depression. This is the most socially destructive pattern of heroin use, potentially drawing in people of a retreatist frame of mind who have few foci of economic and social involvement or pleasure other than the drug. Furthermore these communities are least well served by health and welfare services and the parents and other lay responders to such problems have few material resources with which to conduct any kind of fightback.

Nevertheless, as Donoghoe *et al.* suggest in Chapter 4, difficult circumstances can draw out strong responses. In part of this chapter, these authors describe the way in which women in one metropolitan area in the north of England (many of them mothers of heroin users) utilised and extended existing tenants' organisations to confront local dealers, to demand better state services and collectively to control and care for their young people. More generally, Donoghoe *et al.* describe how family members, mothers especially, respond when they discover that a child of theirs has taken drugs. Initially, there is a period characterised by shock, feelings of disorientation, anger and guilt, followed by discussion within the family and with neighbours and by a variety of strategies of care and control of the wayward young user. In the longer term some families then turn to public forms of action. Several case studies are outlined, showing how – depending upon the social and cultural resources available – parents may organise collectively to attack the problem locally, or may leave it in the hands of state and other services, or may work alongside and with such services.

Although spending on health-system responses to drug problems has increased, these responses have not kept pace with the growth of such problems. In the penultimate chapter, Susanne MacGregor and Betsy Ettorre describe the current state of services, pointing up the changes in balance between the statutory services (Drug Dependency Units, colloquially known as 'clinics') and the non-statutory services, and discuss the limits and possibilities for future developments. The authors see the relationship between statutory and non-statutory systems of care as having passed through several phases. In the late 1960s, the statutory sector was assumed to be adequate to care for and control heroin users and the non-statutory sector was not recognised as capable of making more than a peripheral contribution. Throughout the 1970s, the non-statutory sector became seen as an important adjunct to the statutory sector. During this time, the concerns of policy-makers focused on the need to provide an integrated system of care and control in those areas of Britain in which the heroin problem was then concentrated. In the latest and current phase, services have been extended geographically, in response to the spreading of the problem, through the government's Central Funding Initiative. In many localities, practitioners are becoming more aware of the problems of women and of ethnic and religious minorities, though this awareness is still a rare and fragile thing and is not generally reflected at the policy-making level or in the provision of services. Overshadowing current activities is the knowledge that central government 'pump-priming' through the Central Funding Initiative (CFI) was designed to be a short-term measure intended to stimulate the setting-up of services that thereafter attract local funding. There is considerable uncertainty about the likely pattern of services from 1987 onwards, when the CFI begins to wind down, and prospects for statutory and non-statutory services that are innovative or oriented to special needs do not look particularly encouraging at present.

For a minority of those affected by drug problems, there is the option of private, fee-for-service treatment and rehabilitation. It is no longer novel to observe that middle-class people – even upper-class people – are as prone to using heroin as are other social groups. A high level of disposable income allows easy expenditure on leisure pursuits such as the use of legal and illegal drugs, and we have indicated this possibility in Figure I.1 by the term 'yuppie' ('young, upwardly-mobile') drug use. Nearly every Western political administration has faced the embarrassment of sons or daughters of Ministers or others of high office being exposed as users of illegal drugs such as heroin. Sometimes such exposure has been precipitated only by the event of death through overdose. More generally, heroin use seems quite at home in the middle and upper-middle classes, and provides a fair trade for the purveyors of private treatment.

That heroin problems are to be found at all levels of society is now generally acknowledged. The question, then, is what to do about it? The contributors to the volume examine specific aspects of the problem – supply and enforcement, treatment and rehabilitation, the relationship between socio-economic conditions and heroin problems, family and community responses – and whilst they share a broad perspective upon the nature of these problems they do not constitute a tightly-bounded 'school of thought' with a policy manifesto. This being the case, the editors themselves have attempted to provide a final chapter in which proposals are made for diminution of heroin-related problems. Our general conclusion is that action to prevent production and supply at international level will continue to be only partially effective. The problem must therefore be tackled within Western countries through a mixture of innovative strategies to control distribution (hence, availability and consumption) and 'harm-reduction' strategies building upon the existing practices of a range of practitioners, both professional and lay. Whilst the other contributors to this volume have seen a draft of this final chapter they carry no responsibility for it. If our conclusions are controversial and perhaps not spelled out in as much detail as the reader would wish, then we apologise and plead the case that an outline statement is at least useful as a starting-point for criticism and counter-proposals.

The chapters by Gerry Stimson, Susanne MacGregor and Betsy Ettorre, Geoff Pearson and our other colleagues are prefaced by an initial chapter giving a straightforward description of what heroin is, how it 'works', and what the patterns of use and associated dangers may be, as well as brief, introductory discussions of some issues relating to heroin and crime and to heroin and treatment. This chapter is closely based upon an extended briefing paper prepared by ISDD staff and updated for publication here. For some readers this material may be familiar 'old hat' but we have included it for both theoretical and practical reasons. At a theoretical level, we believe that the social and economic sciences have to recognise the material facts of biology and the body. Practically speaking, accurate knowledge can save lives if it informs policy and practice.

One thing this book does *not* offer. The contributors abstain altogether from the kind of chapter which begins:

From ancient times immemorial Man [*sic*] has sought relief, transcendence and happiness by all manner of means . . .

We hope that this collection is the more immediately relevant (and readable) for this abstention and that it proves of general interest and practical value to all those concerned with issues of health, enforcement, self-help, social welfare and social policy generally.

Nicholas Dorn
Nigel South

1

Heroin today: commodity, consumption, control and care

ISDD Research and Development Unit

'The word narcotic *comes from a Greek word meaning "stupor".
Stupor is a state of reduced sensibility that has given rise to our
familiar adjective* stupid.' (Weil and Rosen, 1983, p. 80)

Heroin is a beige, brown, grey, off-white or sometimes pinkish
powder that is derived from the opium poppy which grows in
many parts of the world. Pharmacological 100 per cent pure
heroin is white, but different manufacturing processes and
additives give it a variety of shades.

Origins of heroin

Heroin is made from the opium poppy – *Papaver somniferum*.
Raw opium is collected from the seed-pods of the poppy by
making incisions in the pods and scraping off the liquid that seeps
out and congeals on the outside. This congealed resin-like
material is mixed with water to which lime has been added,
producing a form of morphine – the intermediate stage between
opium and heroin. The morphine is treated with other chemicals
to produce a precipitate of heroin, which is then dried to produce
granules or powder. Production processes are basically similar
whether the drug is being made legally or illegally.

About 200 kilograms of heroin per year is legally manufactured
in Britain (International Narcotics Control Board, 1984; Home

11

Office Drugs Branch, personal communication, 1984). The bulk of this legally and domestically manufactured heroin is used as a pain-killer in medicine, less than 5 per cent being prescribed as 'maintenance' doses of heroin for some of the addicts attending drug dependency units (Home Office Drugs Branch, personal communication, 1984). The drug dependency units (clinics) have for many years been cutting down on the amount of heroin prescribed, and the amount of heroin being illegally imported has risen, so heroin obtained from clinics now forms a very small proportion of the total amount used for recreational and other illegal purposes.

Most of the heroin used illegally in Britain is imported from countries in south-west and south-east Asia, being produced in small illicit 'kitchen' factories and smuggled into Britain by courier or hidden inside other goods. This heroin – sometimes prepared for smoking and sometimes for injection – may be 'cut' or diluted with other substances after entry into Britain. At the present time the purity of heroin samples remains quite high, averaging between 70 and 90 per cent on entry into Britain (O'Neil, P. *et al.*, 1984, pp. 889–902) and 20–50 per cent 'on the street' (though it may vary considerably from one sample to another).

Availability

Heroin, it is claimed, is available for sale in most towns in Britain (if you know where to go and whom to ask), but this availability probably fluctuates from one town to another and from time to time. In large conurbations and their environs there may be a more ready and stable supply, since several sources of supply will coexist.

Whether the main factor expanding heroin use over the past few years has been the ready supply at international level, the actions of criminal organisations that have increasingly moved into international drug trafficking, illegal 'small business' activity by persons in areas lacking many other economic opportunities, or increased demand for the drug is a matter of contention. Perhaps each of these factors is in some way responsible, but we do not know to what extent. Recently the price of good-quality heroin has dropped, and this may be partly due to economies of scale associated with a larger distribution network for the drug in many parts of Britain and elsewhere. This expansion of the market may be most accounted for by increases in heroin *smoking*, about which we say more later.

The range of effects sought by users

There are four aspects of the effect of heroin that are experienced at the time of taking it.

Pleasure

Heroin users may smoke, snort or inject the drug. Injection may be directly into a vein, into a muscle, or into the flesh just under the skin (which gives a slower diffusion of the drug into the bloodstream). Snorting involves absorption through the membranes in the nasal passages and this also slows down the speed at which the drug reaches the brain, when compared with intravenous injection. Smoking the drug provides a slightly faster route to the brain than injection or snorting, but some smokers may take their dose in stages rather than all at once (which is the standard procedure with injection).

Many heroin users – particularly those who inject directly into a vein – report that they experience a 'hit', 'flush' or 'rush' which is intensely pleasurable. This reaction is related to the initial effect of heroin on the body, and is short-lived. Not everyone experiences the 'rush' as pleasurable, and many new users feel violently sick at about the same time. These feelings of nausea generally subside if the person persists in using the drug.

Those who do persist in using the drug and begin to do so fairly regularly find that they become accustomed to the initial effects (technically, this is an aspect of the body's 'tolerance' to the drug – see below) and they may wish to increase the dose in order to get as much pleasure as they first experienced.

Once it has been taken into the body by injection, smoking or snorting and passed through the blood–brain barrier, heroin has a 'half-life' of only two and a half minutes (meaning that the amount of heroin in the body is halved, then halved again, etc, every two and a half minutes). It is rapidly converted into morphine, which is responsible for subsequent and longer-lasting effects (Stimmel and Kreek, 1975).

Relaxed drowsiness – a mixture of euphoria and tranquillity

Depending upon the dose taken, the user may continue to interact socially in a relaxed manner; or may become more introspective and go 'on the nod' (so called because of the lolling of the head); or may 'crash out' into unconsciousness (potentially dangerous). Most users probably aim for a state of mind which combines continuing consciousness with relaxed feelings, though established users of high doses may crash out following their enjoyment of the initial rush. Those who go 'on the nod' may sometimes be more alert and attentive than they seem, being able to respond rapidly to any sudden change in the situation around them. It is possible that different users pay primary attention to different parts of the experience of intoxication and its aftermath.

Relief from anxiety and pain

In common with other derivatives of the opium plant (opium itself, morphine, codeine) and some synthetic opiate-type drugs (methadone, etc.) heroin may distance the user from physical pain and from psychological states such as fear and anxiety, or alternatively may modify the perception of pain or anxiety so as to make it more tolerable. For as long as the state of intoxication lasts – and this may be several hours, depending upon the dose and other circumstances – so the person will be shielded from the full impact of pain and anxiety.

This property of the drug may be valued by those users who suffer some kind of distress and wish to set it aside, albeit temporarily. Such users, if they become *regular* users, may find withdrawal from the drug and staying off particularly difficult since the loss of the pleasurable effects of heroin will coincide with the *reappearance* of their original distress. Other users, however, who are not initially motivated to take heroin to mitigate distress and who do not learn to use heroin in this fashion (perhaps because they are not very distressed or anxious) will be more likely to focus upon the positive reasons for using. It is perhaps such users who find it easier to use heroin episodically and recreationally at some times and to go without at others. (See subsequent sections for more on dependence and withdrawal.)

Cultural, situational and motivational aspects 'steering' the drug experience

Besides heroin's particular pharmacological actions, the circumstances in which people use the drug will also influence the sorts of experiences that they have when they take it. Not only their *motivations* for using the drug (e.g. for pleasure, to escape pain, for exploration, to be like a friend, or a combination of these and other reasons) but also the immediate *situation* in which use occurs (who, if anybody, is present or may arrive, what activities are occurring, what interpretations of their experiences are offered by others?), and the *culture* or subculture which frames such situations and gives them meaning – all these may play a part in steering the drug effects one way or another.

For example, solitary users may be more likely to go 'on the nod' or go to sleep than people who use drugs in a group involved in conversation or other social activities (though the whole group may become drowsy if this is their preferred experience). Alternatively, people whose main interest is in the initial rush may make efforts to emphasise this and to disregard or overcome the following sedation – perhaps with the aid of stimulants.

The existing drug literature tells us very little about the cultures, situations and motivations informing the drug use of the new wave of young heroin smokers and snorters, about their dose levels or frequencies of use, or about the ways in which these groups seek to 'steer' their drug experiences or the effects they get. Most of our up-to-date information comes by word of mouth from street agencies and other non-statutory and statutory agencies. Such observers speculate that the mode of administration – i.e. smoking or snorting – may have consequences for the drug experience which differ from those of injection. Smoking may to some extent appear to 'normalise' the activity in comparison with injection (which is rare in everyday life and which has medical and other connotations). It has also been suggested that, as the number of people who use or have used a drug increases, so such people become less distinguishable from the general population:

> as notorious drugs (such as use of heroin) become more widespread in a population the people using them are likely to be more normal (statistically and in other senses) than the abnormal population who presented originally. When a city with a couple of million inhabitants has only one or two dozen heroin users then this group will probably be deviant and abnormal in many ways; but as this behaviour becomes more widespread the abnormal characteristics will become less noticeable. By the time there are several hundred thousand drug takers in such a city their characteristics would be much more similar to the non-using population. This is not to say that such changes are not a cause for concern and do not warrant serious consideration and response; it is meant to illustrate that the different status of this group becomes progressively less apparent as the drug-using population increases (Strang, 1984, p. 1204).

The consequences of this possible 'normalisation' – and the circumstances in which it is most likely to occur – are not known. One consequence might be that most drug users have fewer health and social problems, as they no longer identify with 1960s and 1970s stereotypes of the 'messed-up addict' and as extreme public reactions against them lose momentum. It is possible, therefore, that as Britain's heroin problem expands in terms of numbers of ever-users, so the problems of the average user become less serious.

Patterns of use and their consequences

In this section we discuss patterns of heroin use in terms of frequency and regularity of use (that is, users can be regular or episodic users), and in terms of the mode of administration (smoking or snorting, or injection into the skin or veins).

Defining what is meant by 'regular' use is not easy. We take it to mean either daily use (once or more per day) or fairly consistent use at particular times of the week (for example, on particular days, over the weekends, or at some other stable time and place). Occasional or episodic use, on the other hand, is use that occurs less frequently or in no consistent pattern.

Estimates made in the early 1980s of numbers of persons using opiate-type drugs 'regularly' and probably dependent upon them to some extent varied from 25 000 to 40 000, depending upon whether one was interested only in those using at a particular point of time, or those using regularly at some time or another during a given year (Advisory Council on the Misuse of Drugs, 1982). These figures were approximately five times the number of persons then officially notified to the Home Office as being 'addicts' – figures supplied by doctors in drug clinics, prisons, hospitals, general practice and private practice. Most regular users are, therefore, not in treatment. Most regular users throughout the 1960s and early 1970s were injecting the drug (and generally injecting other drugs, including barbiturates and/or synthetic opiates, as well) but from the late 1970s smoking and snorting became increasingly common.

It is possible to smoke or snort regularly or occasionally – though there is always a danger of moving from occasional use to more frequent use (and dependence), and from smoking or snorting to injection. We simply do not know what the likelihood is of such progression within any of the social groups amongst whom heroin smoking has recently expanded.

Regular injection is now probably the least common form of involvement with heroin in Britain – not because it has become less common, but because other forms of use (smoking and snorting) have become more common. The consequences of regular injection fall into two categories:

- consequences of injection as a means of administration (that is, also experienced by occasional injectors), and
- consequences of regular use (mainly, the development of tolerance and almost certain dependence).

Consequences of injection

Injectors, whether regular or irregular users, face three specific consequences not faced by non-injectors.

- In the first place, their mode of administration typically delivers the whole dose into the bloodstream in one batch. Because all the drug goes in at once, it is not possible to regulate the dose in response to felt effects, as is possible in snorting or smoking. Overdose is more likely with injection than with snorting or smoking.

- In the second place, injection carries specific dangers of infection, related to some users' lack of stable housing and other facilities necessary to maintain cleanliness, and to their failure or inability to use sterile equipment and water (in which heroin is 'cooked up' to dissolve it prior to injection). Hepatitis and other infections, including HIV (the AIDS virus) can be passed from one user to another if they share a needle. Veins may be damaged by injection, especially if material not totally soluble in water is injected, as may happen when heroin is adulterated with insoluble material or when other opiate-type and sedative drugs are injected in the absence of heroin or in preference to it.

- Lastly, injection carries certain symbolic aspects (though these may vary from group to group), and not only the users themselves but also non-users aware of their practice may react to injectors in specific ways that mark them off from 'the normal'. Thus the mode of administration may have consequences for how users perceive themselves and their drug use, and hence consequences for their future use of drugs: some injectors may become quite involved in playing at the role of 'addict'.

Heroin presents particular dangers to women. Women's bodies generally and their livers particularly are smaller than men's, and women are thus more at risk of liver damage. Oral contraceptives place a strain on the liver, making it more hazardous for women using such methods of contraception to use heroin. Frequent, regular heroin use causes women's periods to stop, though pregnancy is still possible since other aspects of the menstrual cycle continue. As with other sedatives, heroin passes to the unborn baby and sedates him or her, with the results that growth may be slowed and withdrawal occur at birth (DAWN, 1984, p. 4).

Consequences of regular use

As far as the development of a 'habit' is concerned, two aspects of regular heroin use are significant: the development of tolerance (a physiological phenomenon), and the potential for dependence (a psychological as well as physiological state). Tolerance, as already noted above in the section on drug effects, is the process whereby the user's body begins to adapt to the presence of the drug. Regular, frequent (for example, daily) users generally experience a degree of tolerance. There is some evidence that the development of tolerance varies with the person's circumstances and expectations. High-dose hospital patients, for example, who are given the drug in the context of no history of its abuse, are less likely to experience tolerance than are regular street users. Tolerance to different aspects of the drug's effects develops at different rates, so some users may increase their dose in pursuit of one effect (for example, euphoria) even though the body may not have adapted in other ways. One consequence of the development of tolerance is that users may edge their dose upwards in order to get the same 'rush'. Another consequence is that overdoses may occur if a hitherto regular user stops using for a while and then resumes at their previous dose level.

Dependence means that a person has come to rely upon the drug to feel normal. A person who has become dependent on heroin or similar sedating drugs experiences discomfort ('withdrawal symptoms') if he or she cuts down on the dose rapidly or stops using the drug for a day or two. Withdrawal symptoms, which in their physical aspects resemble influenza, vary in their severity according to the dose of heroin to which the person has become accustomed and according to their expectations and motivations. It should be noted, however, that even occasional users may become dependent on the drug to get them through certain situations or to provide an occasional diversion or reward – there are different kinds of dependence. For a discussion of withdrawal and its management, see Yates (1982) and Blenheim (1983).

Summarising: regular injectors face the greatest dangers of infection, physical (e.g. venous) damage, dependence, and social stigmatisation. They may however develop a degree of practical knowledge and expertise that helps them to minimise some of these risks. Their development of tolerance to drug effects may reduce the chances of accidental overdose for as long as they remain regular users, but if they discontinue heroin use (hence losing their tolerance) and then resume heroin use at their previous dose, they will be at particular risk of overdosing.

Episodic injection

Those heroin users who inject it only occasionally, or in short 'runs' of, say, once a day for a few days, or who inject once or twice a week or less on average but not in any regular pattern – are less likely to suffer some of the adverse consequences of regular users. That is to say, irregular users generally do not develop tolerance, and will not need to increase their dose to get satisfaction (though they may, of course, still choose to move to a higher dose, or drift into doing so). They also run a lesser risk of dependence than do regular injectors, since their bodies do not become adapted to the fairly continual presence of morphine metabolites. They may however find that they have become dependent on the use of the drug at certain times that might otherwise be trying or anxiety-producing. There is a clear risk of progression from injecting a few times to more regular and dependent patterns of use.

Other than this, episodic injectors run all the risks of injection (already mentioned), though less often than regular injectors. Episodic injectors may or may not be in good health generally and in materially and emotionally secure environments, and these aspects are likely to influence their experience of drug use and the consequences for physical and mental health.

There is one respect in which irregular injectors may be at greater risk than regular users. The risk of overdose may sometimes be higher in casual and intermittent injectors because of their lack of tolerance and lack of experience in finding out from their suppliers exactly what (and in what strength) they are taking.

Persons who inject heroin regularly at one time may discontinue at other times – and vice versa. Injectors may, in other words, vary their level of involvement with drugs as time goes on.

Regular smoking or snorting

An unknown number of people smoke and/or snort heroin on a fairly regular basis – once a day, say, or at weekends. Snorting seems to have followed cocaine use in some middle-class circles, while smoking (including 'chasing the dragon') has been widely reported in both working-class and middle-class areas. Until the early or mid-1980s, it seemed to be primarily males who were involved in smoking, but more recent reports from street agencies and other sources suggest that women's involvement has been increasing. (Most recreational drug practices have historically first been taken up by men and then filtered through to women who have used illegal drugs less heavily in many cases.) And, in contrast to the 1970s, some agencies report that they are beginning to be approached by heroin users of Asian and African descent.

Smoking heroin is done by placing the drug on a piece of metal foil or similar object, heating it from underneath until it smokes, and then drawing in the smoke by means of a straw, funnel or like object (this is called 'chasing the dragon'). Alternatively, but less commonly in this country at the present time, heroin or other opiates may be mixed with tobacco or other smoking substance and smoked in a pipe or rolled cigarette. An amount of heroin can also be picked up on the glowing tip of a cigarette. In any case the smoke is drawn into the lungs.

Snorting heroin is done in a manner similar to sniffing other substances such as snuff or cocaine. In this case part of the drug is absorbed by the nasal lining, and hence passes into the bloodstream.

Neither smoking nor snorting heroin carries any major dangers specific to these modes of administration other than incidental dangers of smoking tobacco when the drug is mixed with it. Both methods are less dangerous than injection, in so far as risks specific to injection are avoided.

Regular, frequent use of heroin by smoking or snorting however, does carry with it the probability of developing tolerance, wishing to increase the amounts used, becoming dependent, and suffering discomfort if one does not continue the pattern of use to which one has become accustomed. There may also be social, financial, legal and other problems (see below). There is also the possible danger of switching to injection to maximise the effect, a development that some street-agency staff suggest may occur amongst those who have been smoking heroin regularly and heavily over a year or more.

Episodic smoking or snorting

This is probably the most widespread of all present-day involvements with heroin, yet least is known about it. Of the two modes of administration, it is smoking which is reportedly most widespread. The typical episodic smoker is white, but there is no clear social-class profile. There have been reports of large numbers of such users in inner-city areas of decline and mass unemployment. These reports may be triggered partly by a general concern about unemployed youth and their social behaviour and future development, rather than by any real concentration of heroin users in such areas. In any case, there are also reports of young people from middle-class backgrounds, both employed and unemployed, smoking heroin, so this form of drug involvement should not be linked solely with social deprivation.

It seems more plausible to describe the spread of the practice as one aspect of young people's boredom, desire for excitement and pleasure, involvement in getting hold of the drug by participating in aspects of a petty criminal 'irregular economy', and a willingness to try a drug that can be administered in a way that builds upon existing practices (for example, smoking cigarettes, cannabis). See Auld *et al.* (1986) and Pearson (in this volume) for further discussion.

Summarising the last few paragraphs, we can say that whilst occasionally smoking and snorting heroin carry a range of dangers, these dangers are multiplied by regular use and by injection. But things are more complicated than this. So far we have been talking as if people took heroin pretty much in a vacuum, and as if the consequences of their use of the drug depended solely upon how much they took, by what means and how often. There are other issues that interact closely with heroin use.

Overdoses

One important cause of death amongst users of heroin and other sedating drugs is overdose (Spear, 1983; ISDD, 1986, p. 6). Overdoses are caused by taking too much of a particular drug (e.g. heroin or barbiturates) at one time, or by mixing drugs (taking two or more sedating drugs within the same period of time). The actual cause of death in many cases of overdose is respiratory failure (inability to breathe) because of airways being blocked by vomit inhaled into the lungs.

In some respects regular heavy use of heroin is less dangerous than regular heavy use of barbiturates. This is because tolerance develops to the respiratory depressant effects of heroin but not to those of barbiturates, making it easier for the heroin-overdosed person than for the barbiturate-overdosed person to keep breathing. So a tolerant heroin user who increases his or her dose to overcome tolerance and hence experience the drug's euphoric effects is less likely to die than is a barbiturate user who increases his or her dose of that drug.

Because tolerance is lost if the regular user discontinues drug use for a period of time, such people are particularly at risk to overdoses. Such people may not realise that a spell in prison or a period spent drug-free in treatment and rehabilitation will cause them to lose tolerance, and may therefore re-start drug use at their old dose level, resulting in an overdose. This danger occurs with sedatives generally, not just heroin, and it may be appropriate for professionals such as probation officers and rehabilitation staff to warn clients of it.

Countermeasures

Countermeasures to an overdose by heroin and alcohol, alcohol alone, other sedatives, or a combination of these are quite simple. It is no good giving stimulants (either pills or coffee). If a person is fully conscious, but is suspected of having taken an overdose of sedatives by methods including swallowing, eating or drinking, then s/he should be encouraged to be sick to remove alcohol or other sedative stomach contents. This is however not an entirely safe procedure if the person is not fully conscious and alert, since vomit may lodge in the airways and prevent breathing.

In all cases of suspected overdose – and especially when the person is drowsy, unconscious, or has slow or uncertain breathing or heartbeat – an ambulance should be called to take them to the Accident and Emergency Department of the nearest hospital without delay. Meanwhile, it is essential to maintain an adequate airway, to make sure that their breathing is unrestricted, and to lie them on their side with their head turned slightly towards the floor (so that any vomit has a chance of dropping out of the mouth rather than falling back to obstruct the airways). If in doubt, the safest course of action is to call an ambulance. Standard first-aid resuscitation may be necessary (*Readers Digest*/AA, 1985; Campbell, 1984).

Drug interactions and life-style

Many deaths that occur amongst heroin users are due to their use of a *variety* of drugs, and/or to general neglect and ill health amongst that proportion who take drugs in particularly adverse conditions. Heroin is a sedating drug, as the effects once the initial 'rush' has passed make clear. Alcohol is another sedating drug (as are barbiturates and other hypnotics, major and minor tranquillisers and, broadly speaking, solvents that may be sniffed). When two or more of these drugs are taken during the same period of time, their effects tend to interact to produce a more powerful effect, with consequences that include increased risks of accidents (for example, falling, driving accidents, etc), loss of consciousness and possible death due to respiratory failure.

One American study (of injectors) found that the only factor differentiating a sample of *dead* heroin users from a matched sample of *living* users was the former's heavy use of alcohol (Baden, 1972). It seems likely, therefore, that drinking provides the general or specific conditions in which heroin may be more likely to cause death by overdose. Use of other sedating drugs alongside heroin – such as barbiturates, tranquillisers, and synthetic opiate-like drugs (for example, methadone) – similarly increases the danger of overdose and death, but it is worth emphasising alcohol since it is often overlooked even though it is used quite heavily by many users of illegal drugs (see Rounsaville *et al.*, 1982).

It makes sense, therefore, to warn heroin users of the special dangers of drinking when they are high, and to warn drinkers who are in conditions where heroin is relatively freely available not to use it then. Whilst there is no direct evidence on this point, it seems prudent to assume that smokers and snorters, as well as injectors of heroin, are at risk when drinking or using other sedating drugs.

It should also be remembered that some casualties are the result of a combination of particularly hazardous forms of drug use (for example, injection of a variety of substances) and poor environmental, economic and social conditions. Street agencies and other statutory and non-statutory agencies have evolved a variety of approaches towards helping people in such circumstances (Blenheim Project, 1983; DAWN, 1984; Dorn and South, 1985).

Criminality and heroin

The idea that heroin use leads to crime is put forward today almost as a matter of common sense. The popular argument is that people turn to property crime (and may employ violence) in order to support their heroin habits. The argument was originally applied to American heroin injectors and has recently been extended to young heroin smokers. But the evidence for this idea has always been very 'shaky', and it seems probable that the relationship between drug use and crime is more complex than this:

> There is no evidence that opiates are a cause of crime in the sense that they invariably lead to criminality, but there is no doubt that among those addicts with a delinquent life-style drug use is part and parcel of their other activities, crime included (Research Triangle, 1976).

In what follows it needs to be remembered that, by definition, possession of illegal drugs is itself a crime: we are talking about the relation between this and other forms of criminal behaviour.

British studies of drug users suggest that 'no drug has inherent criminogenic properties' (Mott, 1981). Most males notified to the authorities as addicted to opiate drugs were convicted of offences before being notified. Studies in several other countries also suggest that people typically become involved in petty crime *first* and in heroin *later*. For example: 'Drug addiction is one of the later phases of the criminal career rather than a predisposing factor' (Meyer, 1952). Some young people already marginally involved in non-drug crime may increase such involvements at the same time as they become involved in drug use, but this in itself is not evidence that the drug use *caused* the increase in crime: 'While crime may increase, it may have happened anyway, given the fact that most contemporary addicts are at an age which is also a high risk age for crime' (Greenberg and Adler, 1974).

Income sources

Accepting, for a moment, that not all drug users support their consumption by means of property crime – how *do* they finance themselves? In trying to answer this question it may be useful to look at the results of American studies, since the levels of heroin use and the surrounding social conditions in Britain today are becoming more like those prevailing in inner-city areas of the USA in previous decades. American studies found that the greater part of heroin users' incomes come from sources such as legitimate employment (for some users), unemployment and welfare payments (for the unemployed), and from dealing in illegal drugs themselves: only a small part comes from non-drug crimes such as property crimes. The heavier the person's consumption of heroin, the more likely is he or she to finance some of this consumption through drug dealing, supplying less frequent users. One review observed that 'a significant percentage (probably between 30 and 50 per cent) of the income needed to support large habits is generated within the drug distribution network itself (that is, by buying or selling illegal drugs). Evidence also indicates that a substantial number of heavy users of expensive drugs obtain substantial financial support from family, welfare and employment' (Wardlaw, 1978, p. 89).

As another major review put it: 'It is becoming increasingly clear that drug use is supported through a variety of legal and illegal sources other than predatory, income-generating person or property crime' (Research Triangle, 1976, p. 21). Of these various sources of income, part-time jobs, occasional paid services for jobs such as car-washing or fetching and carrying, and support from family members are likely to be significant for today's younger heroin users who smoke or snort (or even inject) it on an episodic basis.

There is clearly some danger in suggesting to young people that if they have experimented with heroin, then they are expected to begin to steal. Not only would any such suggestion not be justified in terms of the available research – it would possibly promote an increase in petty crime amongst young people who had become aware of the possibility of saying 'I couldn't help it'.

When crime leads to drug use

Although heroin use does not generally *cause* crime (other than by definition, since possession of certain drugs including heroin is illegal unless prescribed) heroin use is often associated – on a statistical basis – with certain kinds of income-generating property crime (that is, there is a positive correlation). This positive relationship may be considered as being made up of two components:

- Past relationship – people with a record of past minor convictions are reportedly more likely to go on to use heroin than those without such convictions. (This relationship held for some heroin users in some countries in past years, and may or may not apply to Britain today.)
- Present relationship – people who currently indulge in property crime (street crime, burglary, fencing, shoplifting, credit card fraud, etc.) may celebrate by buying intoxicants and/or food and other goods for themselves and others whenever their activities bear fruit.

As studies of the problem have put it: 'Persons who are very successful in income-generating crimes may spend a sizeable portion of their income on a luxury good – heroin. Then, does the consumption of heroin lead to criminal behaviour, or does criminal behaviour lead to heroin consumption, or both?' (Research Triangle, 1976, p. 22).

In other words, temporary success in crime may lead to a temporary increase in drug use: crime sometimes leads to drug use.

Weighing up the evidence, we can say that the published literature casts doubt on the idea that the best way of understanding the complex relationships between crime and use of drugs is to say that drug use (heroin or other) typically leads to crime against property or persons (Gandossy *et al.*, 1980).

As regards occasional or irregular users – including many of the younger and occasional smokers – money from legal sources, including family pocket-money, is probably sufficient.

Many frequent users may deal in heroin and/or other drugs at least sometimes, and the income from this together with that from legal sources may be sufficient. When it is not sufficient the user may seek either other criminal sources of income and/or a drug clinic supply of legal heroin (which however is very rarely obtained nowadays) or other opiate-type drug. Alternatively, he or she may cut down the dose and frequency of drug use. There is evidence that the provision of heroin maintenance supplies to clinic attenders reduces the extent of their involvement in crime, though it does not prevent crime altogether (Hartnoll *et al.*, 1980).

The small dealer/user thus has a variety of alternatives to property crime to support his or her consumption, and the occasional dealer/user generally has no need to 'turn to crime' because an occasional and low level of consumption is not so difficult to underwrite from legal sources of income.

This suggests that if one is concerned to identify one or more 'types' of heroin users who are worth looking at in more detail to see if their drug use positively drives them into crime, it might be most fruitful to look at those poorer users who use relatively heavily, yet do not choose (or are for some reason unable) to support their habit partially through dealing in drugs. There is an obvious need for research into such possibilities in the present British situation.

One useful moral would seem to be that just because heroin misuse, petty property crime, and major crimes of drug trafficking are all bad things, this does not mean that they should be confused and regarded as the 'same thing': separate and specific strategies against each, coordinated within a general programme of enforcement and health measures, may be more effective than a muddled crusade against all three. The next few years carry the opportunity to develop such strategies and evaluate them.

Health and welfare responses

In order to understand some of the debates around treatment, rehabilitation and community responses today, it is helpful to look back a couple of decades. During the 1960s and 1970s heroin injection was the typical mode of administration and smoking the drug was much less common. Most users were over 20 years old, male, and restricted to relatively few geographical areas, especially London and some towns in the south-east. The availability of treatment facilities reflected the pattern of use, with the emphasis being upon the hospital-based drug dependency units (clinics) in London. The clinics were brought into being in 1968, with the intention of bringing heroin users into closer contact with the health and welfare system and breaking their links with private doctors, whose sometimes generous prescriptions fed an illegal market in the drug. By assessing clinic attenders and offering them NHS heroin in injectable form and acceptable doses, the clinics initially managed to attract a large proportion of existing heroin users.

By the mid-1970s, however, it had become clear that the clinics had not been fully successful in containing the problem. Various reasons are given for this: some patients sold part of their clinic supply and bought other drugs or goods with the proceeds (just as some patients of private doctors had sold part of their scripts); partly in response to this, clinic psychiatrists had begun to cut down on heroin prescriptions and to offer injectable methadone, oral methadone or just counselling instead; and world supply of heroin increased during the 1970s. As more and more heroin users approached the clinics, the staff (generally consisting of a psychiatrist, nurses and a social worker) increasingly emphasised extended assessment periods to test the would-be patient's 'motivation', and to offer oral methadone for a short period only. Perhaps initial expectations that a clinic supply of heroin would transform sometimes quite delinquent drug users into conformist patients were unrealistic.

The changes that occurred in the health and welfare system in the 1970s were related to the emergence of new and more sophisticated perspectives, stressing social and psychological aspects of dependence as well as physiological dependence. By 1982 the original concept of addiction to a particular drug –

heroin – had been displaced in government reports by a broader idea of a diversity of drug-related problems that might be medical, legal, psychological and so on (Advisory Council on the Misuse of Drugs, 1982; see also the concluding chapter in this volume). This may be considered the theoretical reflection of practical changes in and around the clinic system, with medium- and longer-term opioid maintenance being partially displaced by short-term social casework with multi-drug users.

Residential rehabilitation

'Rehabilitation' is the process of learning to live without drugs. In Britain, rehabilitation agencies are generally residential houses that draw upon philosophies developed in north American drug programmes as well as upon British traditions of 'resettlement' and moral reform. The basic idea common to most drug rehabilitation programmes is that a person will not be able to stay off drugs unless he or she changes in some fundamental manner, and that such change is best brought about by becoming a member of a close-knit group. Rehabilitation communities have clear and explicit house rules, and in some houses residents and staff take part in 'encounter groups' and house meetings in which any departures from the rules are discussed as examples of individuals' immaturity, lack of responsibility and inability to be honest with themselves.

Residents may stay in the house for several months, though it is common for them to 'split' (leave without completing the programme), finding the situation over-demanding and sometimes oppressive (this is sometimes seen as evidence of lack of motivation or honesty by house staff). Some residents develop a pattern of returning and then splitting again several times over a period of years, though some residential houses will be reluctant to take 'splittees' back.

Not all residential houses operate programmes of this kind. A few offer supportive accommodation and the availability of counselling and advice, and a number of others rely at least in part on the residents accepting Christianity. The relevance of the residential communities in relation to the new wave of younger heroin smokers and snorters has yet to be determined.

Street agencies

Another type of agency that grew up alongside the drug clinics was the day centre. These were places open to drug users, including clinic attenders, who had little to do during the day other than get into trouble. There were never more than four day centres functioning in Britain, and three of these folded up in the 1960s and 1970s because of the increasing numbers of attenders who took not just heroin but also a range of other drugs such as barbiturates, amphetamines and alcohol (the 'chaotic multi-drug users').

Today the one remaining specialist drugs day centre – Lifeline in Manchester – deals mainly with drug users diverted from the criminal justice system. (That is to say, they are effectively given a choice between jail and rehabilitation.) The other three day centres evolved into advice centres (sometimes called street agencies) that allow drug users on the premises for relatively short periods of time to get information, help with practical problems such as accommodation, social security or referral to rehabilitation houses, and counselling. The main trends here are an increasing interest in the needs of women and the provision of a range of advisory and training services to professionals working in statutory services such as social work and probation (Dorn and South, 1985).

Non-specialist services

It is increasingly being recognised that users of heroin and other drugs cannot always be handed on to specialist services, if only because those services cannot handle the numbers. And given the realisation of the importance of understanding the person's drug use in the broader context of their involvements with family and friends, work and community, it makes sense for generic case workers such as social workers, probation officers and GPs to be involved. The government has published guidelines of good clinical practice which suggest that all doctors have a role in giving health care (including general health care, counselling, support, and sometimes forms of treatment specific to the drug used) and that there are good reasons for this, quite apart from the fact that there are insufficient specialist drug units to deal with more than a small proportion of problem drug-users. Alan Glanz has recently conducted research into GPs' involvement in treating drug users (Glanz, 1986; see also MacGregor and Ettorre, this volume).

Training is increasingly recognised as important, both for those working within specialist drug agencies, and for generic health, social welfare, and education workers. There is also increasing interest in ways of supporting parental and other community self-help groups concerned with drug use on a local level.

Crisis intervention

At the same time, however, there is a minority of drug users who are so 'messed-up' – both in terms of poor physical health and of behaviour – that they cannot be cared for except by a 24-hour specialist residential house, and yet are not willing or not able to behave in ways acceptable to most rehabilitation houses. Examples include people who use drugs heavily whilst they are homeless, or overdose repeatedly, or act in unpredictable or frightening ways.

At present there is only one short-to-medium-term crisis-intervention residential agency in Britain – City Roads in London. This agency began as a short-term house with the emphasis upon medical care and advice work, but then moved more towards the model of a rehabilitation house, laying more emphasis on counselling and demanding evidence of 'motivation' of clients (Jamieson *et al.*, 1984, pp. 170–1). Most of the people approaching crisis intervention and rehabilitation houses are users of a variety of drugs of which heroin may be one.

A new balance of control policies

At the beginning of the section on health and social responses, we described the setting-up of specialist health facilities for heroin users in the 1960s as being (in part at least) an attempt to discourage the development of an illegal market in drugs. That approach can now be seen to have had little success in the face of changing social, economic and drug-market conditions.

What has happened more recently is a widespread attempt to bolster specialist drug services by means of an expansion of non-

Table 1.1 Shifts in responses to traffickers, small-scale dealers, users, other family and community members from the 1970s to mid 1980s

	Responses to traffickers and dealers in sizeable amounts, and to their agents	Responses to small-scale and occasional suppliers (who may also be users)	Responses to people possessing for personal use (who may also occasionally deal)	Responses to other family and community members concerned with care/control of users
Main foci of control in 1970s:	Prison sentences for those caught. (Traffickers meanwhile develop more sophisticated organisation).	Fines and/or prison sentences. Attempt to differentiate users from dealers.	Clinics and 'rehabs' supplemented by criminal justice system (imprisonment).	Little clear advice except implicit message about referral of users to specialist facilities.
Recent developments in early and mid 1980s:	Longer (exemplary) sentences. Regional crime squads get involved as 'ordinary' criminal gangs turn to dealing. Forfeiture of assets.	Small-scale supply increasingly considered 'serious' criminality.	Government pump-priming of new health service and non-statutory drugs facilities. Non-specialist doctors urged to help.	Media emphasis on drug use as a cause of crime. Government information campaign warns potential users, suggests parents can cope.
Possible future developments	Increasing disclosure by banks of details of customers' accounts?	Uncertain, the expanding network of small-scale dealing has yet to attract clear preventive proposals.	Closer integration of criminal justice, health and community care responses? Funding patterns and policy lead uncertain once pump-priming runs out.	Future policies uncertain: to what extent can heroin be made a family and community problem? How will specific groups respond to opportunity to be a part of a vague 'multi-agency' strategy?

statutory, community and self-help approaches (residential houses, 'phonelines, parents' groups, etc.). Although the statutory drug services are still there, they no longer rely on heroin maintenance as their main therapeutic tactic. Indeed, non-statutory and community resources *outside* the clinic system have replaced heroin maintenance *inside* as the main adjuct to primary health services in the British system of care and control. We cannot say how permanent this shift in the balance of care and control will turn out to be, since this will depend partly on future patterns of funding and partly on shifts in broader social and economic policies.

So, whilst in the enforcement system there have been fresh attempts to deter drug traffickers and suppliers by means of heavier penalties and the threat of forfeiture of their assets (see preceding section on crime), within health and welfare systems there has been a shift in the balance between 'medicinal' (heroin and methadone maintenance) and 'community' (social work plus parents) strategies. One of the broad aims of the government mass media anti-heroin campaigns in 1985/6 and 1986/7 was to encourage parents to take more responsibility for responding to heroin problems (Dorn, 1986, p. 8). Overall, *taking the fields of enforcement and treatment together*, the result is a partial 'de-medicalisation' of the problem, the stimulation of a (still patchy) range of welfare and advice services and, possibly, the strengthening of links between policing and community involvement. How this still-developing continuum of care and control holds up in the face of new patterns of drug use such as more widespread heroin smoking remains to be seen.

2

The war on heroin: British policy and the international trade in illicit drugs

Gerry Stimson

> I would only say, Sir Edward, that certainly I wish you and your Committee well in your studies, and I am here to assist you in any way that I can, because it is a cardinal belief of the Government at the moment, about this problem, that whereas it was the view of governments years ago that the best way to keep the drugs problem under control was to seek to say in every public utterance that there was *not* a drugs problem, that is no longer an acceptable basis on which to proceed and has not been for some time. (David Mellor, Junior Home Office Minister, giving evidence to House of Commons Home Affairs Committee, 1986)

For many years discussions about British drugs policies could be summed up by the catchwords 'treatment' and 'rehabilitation'. Policy-makers, doctors, agency workers, researchers and journalists have looked to the drug user as a focus for policy, object of treatment and help, and for explanations about the nature of drug problems. The 'drugs' problem was seen as a matter of people and their problems: what could be done, for example, to treat users, reduce harm, or encourage people to stop using drugs. These are, of course, admirable aims, for they deal with the real problems that individuals experience.

The limit to this perspective is that it excludes an examination of the related issues of drug production and distribution. To understand drugs in Britain today, we have to look beyond individual use to those features of international and national economics, trade and policy which make possible the widespread production and use of illicit imported drugs such as heroin and cocaine. A first step in understanding the British heroin problem is to examine the links between drugs on sale in British towns

35

today, and the raw product grown by peasant farmers some several thousand miles away.

This chapter will raise questions about supply, about policies aimed at controlling it, and examine some of the limitations to the current British policy response. The chapter will focus mainly on heroin, as it is around the issue of heroin that much of British policy has been shaped.

The medico-centrism of British policy

An understanding of the heroin market has not been aided by the types of debate that have dominated British policy. Until recently British policy took what I term a 'medico-centric' approach to the addict and the treatment of addiction. The medico-centric approach was otherwise known as the 'British system' for dealing with drug problems. The idea that the British did things in a special way inspired many early discussions and it was often American observers who were prominent in this debate. In the 1940s and 1950s Lindesmith (1965) developed the idea in his arguments against the American penal approach, and in favour of a more medical one. It is interesting on re-reading these early comments to see social scientists' contributions to the medicalisation of addiction. The issues were later developed by Schur in *Narcotic Addiction in Britain and America* (1963). Later contributors such as Judson (1973) and Trebach (1982) similarly claimed that the US could learn a lot from the way we did things here: Judson's book for example was subtitled 'what Americans can learn from the English experience'.

There have been many interpretations of this policy, but what is clear is that, in comparison with other countries, the balance swung much more to the medical side than to the legal. From the 1920s until very recently, drug problems were discussed at the policy level, and treated, mainly within the sphere of medicine. We claimed that we treated our addicts rather than sent them to prison. Edwards summed it up by saying that 'A system which sees the addict as someone in need of help is totally to be preferred to one which treats him only as a criminal' (Edwards, 1969, p. 770).

A second feature of the 'British system' was that as well as treating the individual addict, it was seen as beneficial to the broader society. The approach was thought to limit the social problems of addiction by reducing the financial and criminal problems often associated with it. Furthermore, containing the individual addict in a treatment system would help to prevent the spread of addiction. In other words, it was clearly realised that medical treatment had benefits for society as well as, and sometimes instead of, the individual addict.[1]

This medico-centric view of the addict as a patient had economic implications for the heroin market. This was the special emphasis of Schur's analysis, for he clearly thought that if doctors supplied opiates to addicts, then there would be no subculture of addiction and no illegal market. It is worth reading a quotation which summarises his analysis:

> There is practically no illicit traffic in opiates [in Britain], because the legal provision of low-cost drugs . . . has largely eliminated the profit incentives supporting such a traffic. Similarly, as already noted, serious addict-crime is almost non-existent. The addict in Britain need not become a thief or a prostitute in order to support his habit . . . British policy has also inhibited the development of an addict subculture. The addict is not subjected to a continuous struggle for economic survival and for drug supplies, nor need he constantly attempt to maximise his anonymity and mobility. There is relatively little need for group support, and actual contact with other addicts may be slight (Schur, 1965, pp. 154–5).

Schur wrote before the changes in drug use that occurred in the mid-1960s, and his analysis seemed reasonable at the time. But it was not just social commentators who felt that the medical approach curtailed the development of an organised subculture. Such ideas were later elaborated in the post-1968 Drug Dependency Clinic situation, where many doctors and politicians saw that the clinics would be competing with the illegal market and 'prescribing to keep the Mafia out'. Medicine from the late 1960s was seen to be in a functional relation with the illegal market, in which its major task was the social control of drug distribution. What informed the early days of the drug clinics was the idea that addicts would be attracted to treatment by the lure of a prescription, and that doctors would prescribe the right amount – neither too much, for the surplus could be sold, nor too little, because the patient would turn to the illegal market. Consequently the development of illicit dealing would be curtailed.

There was always an alternative model of the drug user, even if it received less attention. This saw the user (or technically, illegal possessor) as a criminal. Whilst professional debate has been about treatment and rehabilitation (the addict as patient), this country has in fact continued a vigorous legal and penal approach to drugs (the addict as criminal). Indeed, the medico-centric approach was always set within a criminal system that penalised non-medically authorised possession, though this rarely received much attention.

The medico-centric position tended to ignore the fact that the non-medical possession of opiates is subject to strict legal penalty, and that numerous other drugs are not part of the medico-centric domain. It also ignored the fact that a continuing – and probably increasing – part of the British response has been through policing, the courts and the prison system. For example, whilst in 1985 about 4300 new patients were seen in drug addiction out-patient clinics, in the same year over 26 000 were convicted or cautioned for drug offences, and nearly 4000 of these were for offences concerned with heroin and cocaine. In that year nearly 6000 people received a custodial sentence for a drug offence. This side of the British response has tended to be neglected by those centrally involved in policy discussions and debate. For example, the main government advisory body, the Advisory Council on the Misuse of Drugs (ACMD) has devoted much more attention to treatment, rehabilitation and prevention, than it has to penal, legal and control issues.

In the 1980s the character of British policy is changing. I have argued elsewhere that British drug policies are in a state of transformation in which medicine is being displaced from its former central role and being replaced by a more extensive and diffuse response involving a broader range of agencies and ideas about drug problems (Stimson, 1987). A stronger role for the state has emerged: a more active role is being played by central government, the debate on drugs is becoming politicised, and there is a new emphasis on law enforcement, with legal and penal measures to control the supply of drugs. This 'war on drugs' is examined in this chapter. But first it is necessary to understand some of the changes that have occurred in patterns of use of heroin since the end of the 1960s.

The heroin market

Over the past twenty years there have been major changes in the extent and characteristics of heroin consumption. In the 1960s heroin use was mainly concentrated in London and the south-east of England with a handful of users in other major cities. Twenty years later (1987) it can be found in most parts of the country, and is no longer confined to urban environments. Whereas it was once a relatively isolated activity engaged in predominantly by rather eccentric/Bohemian/counter-cultural users, it is now fairly common in many parts of Britain and not accompanied by any special view on life.

Let us look first at the number of consumers and how consumption has changed over the past twenty years. It is hard now to believe that in the mid-1960s there were really only a few addicts, many of whom were known by name by Home Office Drugs Branch staff. In 1968, after what had been seen as a major increase in the extent of heroin addiction, the total number of addicts known to the Home Office was only 2782. In 1984 the number was 12 489 (Home Office Statistical Bulletin, 1985).[2]

Estimating the 'real' number of regular users is a matter of speculation, but methods developed by drug-indicators projects (Hartnoll *et al.*, 1985) suggest that official addict notifications in London, at the time of that research, may be multiplied by 5 to give an approximation of the number of regular users (ISDD, 1984, p. 8). Some drug workers estimate that more than that number again may use opiates on an occasional basis.

On the supply side there are three indicators of the size of the market: seizures by police and Customs, purity, and price.

In the mid-1960s there was virtually no smuggled heroin in this country. At that time, supply was mainly of pharmaceutical heroin diverted from legitimate prescriptions and there were virtually no seizures of illegally imported heroin. The first major seizures came in 1971, when 1.14kg were seized. By 1984, the Customs seized 312kg and the police a further 49kg; the total exceeds that seized in the US (Penrose, 1985). In 1985 seizures in the UK were 334kg and 32kg respectively (Home Office, 1985; 1986).

That supply is buoyant is suggested by purity levels. The average purity of samples analysed by the Forensic Science Laboratories in the winter of 1984 was 46 per cent. Customs data also suggests a rise in purity in the past four years (Society of Civil and Public Servants, 1985). There are wide variations, particularly with small quantities which have passed through several levels of distribution and been mixed ('cut') with other substances. Street level seizures varied from 20 per cent to 70 per cent purity in 1984 according to the Office of the Central Drugs Intelligence Unit (1984). The purity level here is much higher than in the USA where it is estimated at between 3 and 6 per cent.

The final indicator of supply is price. In 1984 the Office of the Central Drugs Intelligence Unit reported that it was retailing at around £80 per gram, but with considerable variation by region and size of purchase. It is one of the few products to have fallen steadily in price in recent years. Between 1980 and 1983 the real price of heroin in London, controlled for inflation, is estimated to have fallen by 20 per cent (Lewis, 1985). This reflects world-wide price changes: the United Nations Commission on Narcotic Drugs (1985) estimates that allowing for inflation and exchange rate fluctuations, illicit heroin prices fell by about 25 per cent between 1980 and 1983. In these inflationary times, there can be few other commodities that have had such dramatic price falls.[3]

The main change in the pattern of supply in the past twenty years is from a distribution that was locally supplied, casual and fairly loosely structured, to the establishment of a more systematically organised market with fairly regularised supply and distribution. In other words, in these twenty years we have seen the development of a heroin market. No one can know the size of this market nor how much heroin is consumed each year in Britain. Some idea of the scale of the market is essential, as we shall see later, in judging the impact of the 'war on heroin'. A simple market-research approach to estimating market volume would take estimated numbers of regular and casual users and estimates of typical consumption as part of the calculation. With current estimates of upwards of 60 000 regular users, and many more casual users, it is likely to be in the region of 3000kg, or 3 tons. That amounts to about 8kg every day.[4]

Law and order and the 'war on drugs'

This is the context for recent policy changes. Clearly, the pattern of drug use in this country has changed dramatically from the days of Schur's commentary. We can no longer accept the argument that the medicalisation of addiction prevents the development of drug cultures and markets. The late 1960s medical view of the social control of addiction, suggesting a functional and competing relation between medicine and the illegal market is also no longer tenable. Medicine gave up this fight in the 1970s. The displacement of medicine from its former central position is occurring as a new debate on drugs is emerging.

Since 1984 there has been an unprecedented level of central government interest and activity in the drugs field. This is the first government to have viewed drug taking as a serious issue, as indicated in David Mellor's quote at the start of this chapter. It has set up collaborative machinery at ministerial level (a recognition that the issues cut across government departments). Drugs policy is no longer of concern to just the DHSS and the Home Office, but also to Customs and Excise, Department of Education and Science, Foreign and Commonwealth Office, Overseas Development Administration, Ministry of Defence, Department of the Environment, Scottish Office, Welsh Office and the DHSS Northern Ireland (Home Office, 1986). This Ministerial Group on the Misuse of Drugs has developed a strategy on drug problems, and the government has put large amounts of money into law enforcement, and into educational, preventive and treatment projects (see Chapter 5 by MacGregor and Ettorre).

The Prime Minister's interest, numerous ministerial statements, reports from the House of Commons Home Affairs and Social Services Committees, and ministerial visits to producer-countries indicate that the area for debate has shifted away from 'drug experts' and that centre stage is for the moment held by government and Parliament. With statements from politicians in other parties, such as David Owen's speech on unemployment

· and drugs (Owen, 1985), and the inclusion of drugs in Labour's new statement on health (Labour Party, 1986), it would appear that drugs, for long neglected as issues for political debate, have now been politicised (cf. Dorn and South, Chapter 6). We are likely to see drugs in all party manifestos at the next election.

The present Conservative government has put drug control on the agenda as a public and political issue, and made it an important part of government policy. There has been a major injection of funds into treatment, rehabilitation, education and prevention: many 'drug workers' would not be in post today but for this money. The comparatively large funding has even led to complaints from experts in the underfunded areas of alcohol and tobacco problems (British Medical Journal, 1986).

The argument in this chapter is about the relative emphasis in policy and funding given to different sectors of the response. Evidence that there has been a shift in the debate and response can be found first in the overall description of government strategy. The key document is *Tackling Drug Misuse: A Summary of the Government's Strategy* (Home Office, 1985 and 1986). There are five aspects to this. Listed in the order they are presented, they are:

(a) reducing supplies from abroad
(b) tightening controls on drugs produced and prescribed here
(c) making policing more effective
(d) strengthening deterrence
(e) improving prevention, treatment and rehabilitation.

The major part of *Tackling Drug Misuse* is devoted to measures to control the supply of drugs. These include supporting international efforts to curb the production and trafficking of drugs by financing enforcement and crop limitation projects, and by promoting international cooperation on enforcement; strengthening Customs and police enforcement through additional staff and recorganisation; tightening the controls on drugs produced here so that there is no 'leakage' to the illicit market; deterring drug traffickers and dealers by high maximum penalties, and by depriving them of the proceeds of their crimes. Second, there is the expenditure on different areas. It is difficult to calculate expenditure on enforcement, because apart from particular international projects, cash sums are rarely specified (unlike the case of new educational, treatment and rehabilitation projects). However, it seems likely that the expenditure on international efforts, Customs and police work, the legal system, and imprisonment, must far exceed expenditure on other areas of the response to drug problems.

Third, evidence is found in the changed nature of the debate. It is typified by the report of the Home Affairs Committee (1985) which argued that the Royal Navy and the Royal Air Force should help the Customs and the police. The committee, chaired by Sir Edward Gardner, called for intensified law enforcement efforts, sequestration of the assets of drug traffickers, extradition of suppliers from other countries, a reform of the banking laws to trace drug money, more efforts for crop substitution and eradication, and an increase in the penalty for systematic dealing in drugs to 'no less than the penalty for premeditated murder'. This was echoed when the Prime Minister, Margaret Thatcher, visited the Customs at Heathrow and the Central Drugs Intelligence Unit at Scotland Yard. She made it clear that there was now a war on traffickers and smugglers, and warned 'We are after you. The pursuit will be relentless. We shall make your life not worth living.'

The medico-centric view included a weak economic version of drug markets (focused on the local drug 'scene', the Mafia potential, and the effect of competitive prescribing). This new strategy also has economic implications, drawing on what we might call a criminal–economic model. The guiding assumption is that old familiar 'guilty pushers' and 'victims' model. The pusher in mind is not so much the local user-dealer (though in the end this is where most enforcement effort is probably expended): rather it is some major criminal entrepreneur. The trade in heroin is seen to be conducted by evil, criminal men, who exploit human weakness. Hence this market has to be regulated by criminal and penal means.

The 'war on drugs' metaphor neatly sums this up. During the 1986 debate on the Drug Trafficking Offences Bill the Home Secretary, Douglas Hurd, referred to the Bill as a sharp new weapon in the fight against drug smuggling. He talked of the world as being 'awash with drugs'. The Home Affairs Committee referred to the 'flood of hard drugs', and described it as the 'most serious peace-time threat to our national well-being'. Similar descriptions abound in this short report:

> Western society is faced by a warlike threat from the hard drugs industry. The traffickers in hard drugs amass princely incomes from the exploitation of human weakness, boredom and misery. The war has never been openly declared and the drug traffic infiltrates insidiously into Western countries . . . the ruthlessness of the big drug dealers must be met by equally ruthless penalties once they are caught, tried and convicted . . . The American practice, which we unhesitatingly support, is to give the courts Draconian powers in both civil and criminal law to strip drug dealers of all the assets acquired from their dealings in drugs. Drug dealers must be made to lose everything, their homes, their money and all that they possess which can be attributed to their profits from selling drugs (Home Affairs Committee, 1985, pp. iv–v).

The effectiveness of the law enforcement response

The rhetoric of the 'war on drugs' has dramatic appeal and captures the public imagination. But what is the nature of the task? Is it possible to stop or slow the supply of heroin to this country? Just what are the problems facing any country trying to control drug importation? What is the impact of measures to control the supply of drugs?

The questions require examination of drug production, importation and distribution within this country; of resources put into intervention measures at each of these levels; and some measure of the 'return' on these resources. We shall start in producer-countries, and follow through to distribution within this country.

Intervening to control production

Supply starts in some poor country. Heroin is derived from opium and all the countries producing opium illicitly on a large scale are underdeveloped (Third World) countries (Lewis, 1985,

p. 18). The evidence from seizures indicates that 85 per cent of the heroin currently coming to Britain originates in Afghanistan and Pakistan, with the rest coming from South-east Asian countries such as Burma, Thailand and Laos, and from the Middle East (Penrose, 1985). The main supplier areas have changed over time – for example, in earlier years it was South-east Asia, then Iran. The prominence of supply countries relates less to geographical proximity (although Mexico is a main supplier of heroin to the US) than to crop success, political conditions, enforcement activity, and cultural and economic links between supplier and supplied countries (Lewis, 1985; Penrose, 1985; UN Commission on Narcotic Drugs, 1985). World opium production from these areas was estimated at between 1423 and 1913 tons by the UN Commission on Narcotic Drugs in 1983.

Opium growing provides a major source of income to many poor farmers. A peasant farmer in Pakistan might devote an acre to opium, producing about 7 kilos which, depending on the success of the crop that year, sell at between £22 and £100 a kilo. The considerable variation in yield is related to soil, density of planting, irrigation and weather (Davies, 1984). South-west Asia has higher yields than South-east Asia. Opium growing is labour-intensive, and the size of the crop is limited by the supply of labour and the need to put some land over to foodstuffs. Depending on quality, 10 kilos of opium make approximately 1 kilo of heroin. Opium is converted to heroin in simple refineries. Patterns of refining have changed since the days of the French Connection when much of this occurred in Mediterranean laboratories. Refining has shifted to producer-countries, with resultant cost and transportation advantages. The local wholesaler in Pakistan sells it for export at about £3000–£4000 a kilo.

Estimates of total illicit production are difficult: satellite surveillance can identify the crop, but yields, as already noted, are variable. The UN Commission on Narcotic Drugs in 1983 estimated opium production for Afghanistan at 400–575 metric tons; Iran, 400–600; Pakistan, 63; Burma, 500–600; Laos, 30–40; and Thailand, 30–35 (Lewis, 1985).

Since the 1970s, there have been many attempts by Western countries to persuade producer-countries to cease growing opium. This has had some success with recipients of US funds in the 1970s, but less in South-west and South-east Asia. Three approaches have been tried; crop eradication, law enforcement and crop substitution.

Crop eradication Crop eradication involves burning or spraying the growing plants. The difficulty with this approach is that these areas are often beyond the reach of government. In the so-called 'Golden Triangle' of South-east Asia the growing areas are controlled by tribal warlords or anti-government rebels; in the so-called 'Golden Crescent' region of Afghanistan and Pakistan many of the growing areas are controlled by fiercely independent tribal groups. These areas are poorly policed, inaccessible and hostile to government officials and to officials from other countries. The US Drug Enforcement Agency has twenty officials in Pakistan, but mostly in the cities rather than the growing areas. Visits to some of the growing areas can only be undertaken with heavily armed guards.

Law enforcement The second approach is law enforcement to prevent people from growing, distributing and refining. For example, the UK has contributed £180 000 to support law enforcement in Pakistan, and has provided additional vehicles for the Pakistan Narcotics Control Board. Law enforcement faces the same problems as crop eradication.

Crop substitution The third approach is to encourage crop substitution, persuading farmers to grow other crops such as sugar beet, fruit or grain crops. This is sometimes accompanied by rural development schemes to develop a new local infrastructure. For example, again in Pakistan, the UK is contributing to a planned five-year crop-substitution and rural-development scheme in the Dir District of the North-west Frontier province of Pakistan. The problem here is that growing-areas are often a long way from markets for these crops, transport is difficult, and the cash returns are much lower. No other crop returns as great a yield as the opium poppy in these conditions.

Whilst law enforcement, crop eradication and substitution are extremely difficult, programme-implementing agencies claim that they are not unsuccessful. In Pakistan it was estimated that opium production was 800 tons in 1979, and this was down to an estimated 63 tons in 1983. Pakistan now claims that much of the heroin emanating from there has been refined from opium grown in neighbouring countries.

It is also no coincidence that the main opium-growing areas have been and remain, politically unstable areas, dependent on trafficking bands, tribal groups and private armies for border security. Western governments have often supported these people as a buffer against communism. This was certainly the case with CIA support for tribal and military groups in South-east Asia, for the groups that controlled opium production were also in military control. It probably also partly accounts for the reluctance of Pakistan and Western governments to disrupt opium-growing and distribution in the border region with Afghanistan. Further, opium growing in Afghanistan is controlled by anti-government and anti-Soviet tribespeople who use opium revenue to finance their armed struggle. Political interests often run contrary to the aims of drug control, as also noted in the final chapter in this volume.

It has been the case that many people in drug-producing countries do not share Western governments' views on the need to control a traditional crop which brings in money. However, there is some evidence that this view is changing since the recent growth of internal heroin markets, in contrast to traditional and less extensive patterns of use of cannabis and (raw) opium. Drug production in the Third World relies on poverty, suitable climates, and an abundance of labour. Drug production provides some additional income to poor peasants. However, the romantic view of the 'happy peasant' working to produce a traditional crop is also misleading. Peasant farmers are exploited just like most growers of raw materials for export. The main profits are made at the refining and export levels. These profits are often taken out of the country, and rarely benefit its economic development. Drug production reproduces the traditional exploitation of poor countries producing raw materials for world markets.

Analysts of cocaine and marijuana production in Central and South America have argued that some national economies are distorted by drug production. Bolivia, a main producer of cocaine is a prime example. It is estimated by Bolivia's Interior Minister that 50 per cent of the country's export earnings come from cocaine (*Guardian*, 1986a). Bolivia is not alone in relying heavily on earnings from drug exports. As for cannabis, it is estimated that it contributes more to Jamaica's foreign-exchange earnings than all other exports combined (Malyon, 1985, p. 64). Some writers have used the concept of 'narcocracy' to describe a political system whose principal economic activity is the production of illicit drugs. Henman argues that the informal narcocracy is becoming a predominant form of social and political organisation in Latin America (Henman, 1985, pp. 140–57). It is not clear how appropriate this concept is for South-west and South-east Asia. It probably applies to conditions in some sub- or cross-state regions, but not to these countries as a whole. It indicates however that drug production cannot be seen as being divorced from the economic and political circumstances of producer countries; indeed drug production may play a part in shaping those circumstances.

Intervening to control importation

The next stage of the journey taken by heroin is when it is smuggled into the consumer countries. Little is known about the structure of importation. From reports of major seizures it appears that importers include 'professional' criminals who are involved in several importations, and also business people who may indulge in one-off importations.

Attempts to control importation are a Customs responsibility. Indeed, the Director of Customs has stated that 'Drug smuggling is the top priority of the Department' (Home Affairs Committee, 1986, p. 67). There has been little research on the policy, strategy and effectiveness of Customs work, but it is possible to delineate some of the parameters of their task. In 1985, 42 million passengers arrived in the UK from foreign destinations. The peak volume at Terminal 3 at Heathrow Airport is 4000 passengers per hour (Rigby, 1985) and it is estimated that as few as 1 in 100 are searched. The person who brings in heroin could be acting independently but is more likely a courier, receiving £1000–£3000 for the trip. The importer is paying about £6000 per kilo of heroin including import costs, so if several couriers are sent through, and one is caught, the loss of heroin is a relatively minor cost against the profits that are made. That kilo of heroin will sell for about £20 000 at the next level of distribution.

The problem of intervening at the level of importation stems not only from the number of passengers, but also from the number of motor vehicles, ships, aircraft and postal traffic – for example, there were 1800 postal seizures of drugs in 1985. There is an increasing use of commercial freight to bring in large consignments. Customs policy is that only 2 per cent of European Community goods are subject to random searches, and in 1983 only 6 per cent of total freight brought into the UK was examined. On the south coast there are thousands of boats, many capable of sailing to other countries. The Society of Civil and Public Servants, pressing a claim for more Customs staff, reports that on a Sunday night up to sixty yachts on the Hamble may report their arrival from abroad and a similar number not bother. There are not enough Customs officers to deal with those asking for Customs attention. The numbers of Customs staff involved in first-line duties – inspection of passengers, vehicles and goods – has been reduced as part of this government's overall reduction in civil service staffing (Home Affairs Committee, 1986, pp. 72–3; Society of Civil and Public Servants, 1986).

Most seizures – probably around 80 per cent – come from random searches, but quantities are small, and are likely to hit the one-off independent rather than the large-scale importer. Many random seizures of small quantities of cannabis are now dealt with by the Customs 'compounding' powers, the payment of an immediate monetary penalty in lieu of prosecution (Godfrey, 1984). Such cases are considered to be too time-consuming for officers to pursue through the courts.

Contrary to popular views, random searches are not the main thrust of the Customs effort. Much of the work is in the area of intelligence. The Customs have over 200 investigators who are now specially assigned to drugs, with government plans for an increase to about 300 by 1987 (*Hansard*, 1985). About eighty work on heroin (Rigby, 1985). Drug investigations now form the major element of the work of the Customs Special Investigation Division. They work in this country and in producer-countries. The UK has now stationed a Customs official in Pakistan, and two are due to be based in India (*Observer*, 1986). International collaboration comes through Britain's membership of the International Customs Cooperation Council which allows for international cooperation against drug-smuggling and connected financial operations (Rigby, 1985). Some of the most spectacular seizures occur from this work – a recent seizure of 40kg of heroin at Felixstowe docks was found in a shipment of brassware from Pakistan.

Despite such successes, the Customs admit that they have a difficult job. In 1985 the Customs seized 334kg of heroin (up from 312kg the year before) (Home Office, 1986). The average size of seizures has risen from 0.523kg in 1979 to 1.487kg in 1984 (Society of Civil and Public Servants, 1985) but as the Home Affairs Committee admitted 'no amount of law enforcement can stop the great bulk of supplies getting through'. Seizures have certainly increased, but probably remain proportionally minimal compared with that which does get through. The Chief Investigation Officer for Customs and Excise, Richard Lawrence, is reluctant to estimate success rates, but no law-enforcement agency anywhere in the world credibly claims more than a 10 per cent interception rate.[5]

Finally, there is the problem of the balance between Customs' inspections and the demands of international travel and trade. There have been considerable pressures in recent years for Customs authorities throughout the world to speed up the movement of goods. As Norman Godfrey, Director of the Customs Directorate puts it, 'there are limits to what it is reasonable to expect the travelling public and the trading community to accept' (Godfrey, 1984). In his evidence to the Home Affairs Committee he described the Customs as being pulled in different directions between the demands to facilitate tourism by reducing controls, and the demands for stricter controls against drug- and other smuggling. Later he stated in reply to a question about lorry searches:

It is certainly true that the level of complete turn-out of lorries at Dover and, indeed, at any port is somewhat restricted. The reason is quite simple: that if we tried to turn-out a very high proportion of the vehicles going through Dover, the port of Dover would very quickly come to a standstill (Home Affairs Committee, 1986, p. 68).

Intervening at the level of distribution within Britain

The next step in the supply of heroin is distribution within this country. Just as little is known about smuggling and the nature of the Customs effort, little is known about the structure of drug distribution within this country or the nature of police strategy and effectiveness.

As to the nature of the distribution system, the best description we have at the moment comes from Lewis (1985, pp. 47–8):

> It is hybrid in the sense that it is neither truly competitive nor completely monopolistic. Relatively concentrated at the import level, it becomes increasingly dispersed as the product flows downwards through a series of sub-levels. At each level there is a mark-up between buying and selling price, representing expenses, time expended, labour costs, overheads, relative risk in relation to arrest, theft or fraud, as well as a return on capital. Security considerations ensure that distribution units at each level are small, comparatively isolated and restricted in access . . . The dispersed and fragmentary nature of the retail heroin market is such that it is unlikely that any single group or cartel could ever dominate the domestic delivery system from top to bottom.

The response to this is a police responsibility, with some Customs involvement at higher levels. The police response is at three levels. All uniformed and plain-clothes officers deal with drug offences which arise in the normal course of duties; every police force in the country (bar one in Scotland) now has a drugs squad which, with the CID, deal with more serious cases; and Regional Crime Squads cover drugs cases crossing more than one police area. In 1983 RCSs had their terms of reference changed to allow them to undertake major drug inquiries and it was soon found that the investigation of drug offences or drug-related crime had become a major part of their work, to the detriment of other police work (Pead, 1984). In July 1983, Leon Brittan, at that time Home Secretary, followed up a recommendation of the Association of Chief Police Officers and announced that RCSs would be strengthened by the addition of dedicated drugs 'wings' and by an increase of more than 200 officers (Penrose, 1985). In 1986 there were over 1200 police officers in force drugs squads and in the Regional Crime Squads with a major commitment to drugs work (Home Affairs Committee, 1986, p. 56).

Intelligence for these activities is provided at New Scotland Yard by the recently created National Drugs Intelligence Unit, which replaces the Central Drugs Intelligence Unit, and is staffed by both police and Customs. An indication of the seriousness with which the Home Office now views drug distribution is the fact that the coordinator, Colin Hewett, has previously headed the Metropolitan Police Special Branch and Anti-Terrorist Squad. As Leon Brittan put it when he announced the new appointment 'In drugs, as with terrorism, the need for good intelligence is paramount'. The presence of both police and Customs is necessitated by the need for cooperation in investigations and apprehensions – for example, with the technique of the 'controlled delivery' where a consignment of illicit drugs is detected in freight or unaccompanied baggage, in circumstances where it is possible for those goods to go forward under the surveillance of police and/or Customs with a view to identifying those responsible for the smuggling (Cutting, 1984).

At an international level, the main vehicle for collaboration is Interpol. The Drugs Sub-Division, which is the largest unit in Interpol, monitors and responds to information about drug enforcement, analyses intelligence, and does drug liaison work and training (Leamy, 1983).

What is the comparative return on this effort? The police make many more seizures than the Customs (3000 seizures of heroin in 1985) but the seizures are much smaller. In weight, the total police seizures amount to only 10–15 per cent of those of the Customs. Despite attempts to move up the chain of supply, the majority of convictions are at the user and user–dealer end: in 1983 for example, two-thirds of police seizures were for less than 1 gram.

New initiatives include a telephone hotline – Scotland Yard's Drug Information line – started just before Christmas 1984, whereby members of the public may inform on suspected drug dealers. Other police forces have followed this initiative, and Customs has launched a similar scheme. Many police areas now use cautioning for offenders caught with small amounts of drugs.

Recent government proposals provide for new control measures and penalties. Parole has been removed for major drug traffickers, and the maximum penalty for trafficking in Class A drugs such as heroin has been increased from 14 years to life imprisonment. It is unlikely that this will deter major importers while profits remain high. The structure of drug distribution makes it difficult for police to gain information on such people. Deterrence seems to be influenced more by probability of arrest than by the penalty. Nor will it be much use in persuading people to inform on those higher up the levels of distribution: for them it may be a choice between a life sentence in prison and a death sentence from a major importer.

Sequestration of assets is another change. New legislation means that drug traffickers can be deprived of their assets. It is hoped that this will take some of the profit out of trafficking. The Drug Trafficking Offences Act deals with seizures, upon conviction, of drug traffickers' assets. It provides new powers for tracing and freezing assets, and for a confiscation order to be imposed on a person convicted of a drug-trafficking offence. Some banks have begun scrutinising customer accounts (*Guardian*, 1986d).

This issue is not being pursued by Britain alone, the idea having been around for some time and already being practised in some countries. In 1983 the Council of Europe Cooperation Group to Combat Drug Abuse and Illicit Trafficking in Drugs (the Pompidou Group) recommended that each EC country should promote the tracing, freezing and confiscation of assets from drug trafficking, and suggested ways of increasing cooperation between countries in such matters. The UN Commission on Narcotic Drugs recommended early in 1984 that such measures be pursued in member states (*Bulletin on Narcotics*, 1984).

Sequestration may be one way of increasing the costs of heroin distribution, and make heroin a less attractive proposition to criminals. The problem is that it requires international cooperation in monitoring the flow of capital, and tighter national controls. The government's current policies on free exchange control militate against this. Indeed international 'money laundering' is not unknown amongst legitimate financial concerns.

The police will also need considerable additional new expertise, including officers with experience of company law, international financing, asset tracing, offshore banking, and other activities such as commodity broking. The task of tracing drug money is so complex that some police commentators believe that it is almost impossible to bring a successful prosecution against major international drug dealers. By establishing a number of companies and bank accounts in the Channel Islands and the Isle of Man, it is possible to finance drug operations in Third World countries, and to hide the proceeds offshore. During the whole operation a British financier will not personally own identifiable assets within the jurisdiction of the British courts (Bosworth-Davies, 1985).

What is likely is that sequestration will be successful against low- and intermediate-level dealers, and not at the higher level, the latter having greater resources for covering and defending themselves.

The effectiveness of control measures

What can be made of all this effort? Earlier it was estimated that the total market for heroin was 3000kg in the UK. Against this in 1984 361kg was seized by Customs and police, and 368kg in 1985. At best, resources put into Customs and police work resulted in the interception of perhaps 10 per cent of imports. This is a 90 per cent failure rate. Seizures, and interventions in producer-countries seem to have had little or no impact on supply. The Society of Civil and Public Servants concludes that at current levels of staffing:

> The large quantities of heroin and cocaine seized by HM Customs and Excise have had no effect on price and purity. This indicates a plentiful supply. Further, the continuing low price and continuing high purity level has happened at a time when the demand has increased rapidly. This increase in demand is indicated by the increased number of addicts notified. It can only be concluded that the supply of hard drugs is more than matching the market (Society of Civil and Public Servants, 1985).

An equally pessimistic assessment was made by the head of the Metropolitan Police Drugs Squad:

> In recent times, by reference to the performance indicators of seizures of drugs and arrests of traffickers and users . . . we have done well and are improving, but by reference to the more appropriate indicators of street price and purity levels,

and the Addicts index – we are not doing at all well – in fact we are doing badly – street prices of heroin and cocaine have come down and at best remain steady and purity levels have gone up (Penrose, 1985).

This very much reflects the world picture. The United Nations Commission on Narcotic Drugs (1985) reported that world-wide seizures of heroin doubled to 12 metric tons from 1982 to 1983 with no impact on price at wholesale or retail level.

Could things be done differently? What if the state allocated more resources to policing and Customs work? Mrs Thatcher has said that the work of Customs must not be hampered by lack of resources and that 'The taxpayer will find the money'. However, despite these strong words of support, it is inconceivable that any government, especially one committed to limitations on public expenditure, could put enough money into this area to reduce the amount of heroin imported to an appreciable extent. Even a doubling of seizures, if nothing else changed, would mean that 80 per cent were getting through. And increased seizures are really only a small additional cost to the importer that can be countered by increasing supply, reducing quality or raising price.

Government ministers are pessimistic. The Social Services Secretary, Norman Fowler, told an international conference of health ministers in London in 1986 that the supply of illegal drugs had not diminished, despite many successes against traffickers. The failure, he said was 'a fact we must face' and called for further international action. Home Secretary, Douglas Hurd, in the debate on the Drug Trafficking Offences Bill said, 'I would be quite wrong if I did not warn that the drugs problem in the UK could well continue to get worse before it gets better . . . [And] we can reasonably expect price and purity levels to remain fairly static' (*Guardian*, 1986b; 1986c).

Policy options – the issues and the questions

It is clear that we cannot understand drug use just at the level of consumption, and that there can be no adequate response limited solely to the consumption-related categories of prevention, education, treatment or rehabilitation. The alternative conceptualisation, promoted in the government strategy, of seeing the problem as predominantly a matter of crime, and the response in mainly legal and penal measures, incorporates an understanding of many of the issues concerning both supply and demand but in turn fails because it deals inadequately with the complexity of the international and national economics and politics of drugs.

One response to the complexity of the task is the libertarian stand that there should be no controls – that there should be free availability. This view is based either on the premise of a 'right to use' or on the argument that most of the problems stem not from drug use but from the control measures themselves. One of the difficulties with this is that all societies control the use of psychoactive drugs in one way or another. If the libertarian appeal is to the abolition of *formal* controls, in the hope that adequate informal controls will emerge, the evidence is that many societies have been unable to develop an equable relationship with psychoactive drugs. This is not to deny that informal social controls are important, for informal regulation occurs with all drugs. In the case of heroin, such informal controls probably prevent most people from developing a dependency or other problems with their drug use. This area, however, is little researched.

At the other extreme is the view that drug use should be totally prohibited, as at present. The problem here is that no state has been successful in this task, however punitive the measures used. In this country we have seen that despite large resources allocated to Customs and policing, and introduction of very high penalties, the heroin market has expanded. With a combination of poor producer-countries, and a high demand for heroin at home, Customs and police efforts cannot stop the import of heroin; at best they slow it down. Against this must be set the undoubted (but difficult to assess) deterrence effect – without controls, it is likely that imports would have been much higher. Here, comparative studies of states and regions which have attempted to deregulate heroin would be of interest.

Somewhere between these positions is the medico-centric approach that was once central to the British response. Controlling the drug problem by treating the addict medically was an option when numbers were small, but, despite calls for a return to the clinic maintenance system, is probably both unworkable and undesirable in the present circumstances.

There is no alternative but to take the control issue seriously. Academic debate on policy options has been scarce, and many practitioners have been prepared to ignore these problems. There is an urgent need to raise the level of policy debate, to review policy options, and to ensure that at a local level, enforcement issues are on the agenda. A number of points might be part of this debate.

First, the need to clarify the overall aims of policy. When we move from the relatively safe areas of treatment, rehabilitation, prevention and education, few (apart from government and control and law enforcement agencies) have clear ideas of what they would want from a control policy. What would be the overall aim? Are we correct in assuming that it would be less heroin, less harm, and fewer users?

Second, if the free availability of dangerous drugs is unacceptable, then controls over supply and use are inevitable. But if total prohibition is unattainable, the question is what sort of limitations there should be. The debate then concerns the acceptable, effective and efficient means of limiting supply. We have various models to work from : alcohol, tobacco, therapeutic drugs, and illegal drugs are subject to different regulatory mechanisms. There is agreement in all cases that regulation cannot be left to market forces. There is divergence and disagreement about strategies.

Third, what are the consequences of the aims and strategies? All policies have costs and benefits to different sectors. At an international level, policy and strategy must respect and benefit needs of both producer- and recipient-countries. At a local level, strategies will have various implications: for example, aggressive enforcement aimed at reducing local supplies, if successful, will force up price. This in turn may reduce availability and hence in turn reduce the numbers of new users: but on the other hand it increases financial costs to regular users and may thereby exacerbate other problems.

Fourth, how will a control strategy relate to other elements of a drug strategy, for example, in the fields of prevention, education, treatment and rehabilitation? From the point of view of social and medical workers the user is a client or patient, but to the police the user is a criminal. What problems arise from these conflicting positions?

Fifth, there is a need to take a long-term view. Some of the conditions for drug production are engendered by the poor positions of producer-countries in the world economic order. In the long run, drug production is related to development issues, which are in turn related to a restructuring of that economic order so that some countries are not kept rich at the expense of the poor. The history of former drug-producing countries, such as China and Yugoslavia, suggests that drug production diminishes when there are major economic, political and social changes.

The desire for long-term changes should not allow us to evade the question of the direction for policy in the short term. In the meantime, what about the existing effort? What of the first link, the producer-country? It is often said that crop-control schemes have failed, but there is room for a more vigorous and imaginative approach. World-wide, the total budget for the United Nations Fund for Drug Abuse Control (UNFDAC), the body through which schemes are pursued, was only $6.8 million in 1983 (Malyon, 1985). The UK contributes £100 000 to the UNFDAC general budget and in 1986 pledged £3.4m for assistance to Pakistan, spread over five years (Home Office, 1986) but, of course, the bulk of UNFDAC contributions does not go directly to the farmers. (it is spent on road-building, irrigation works, other infrastructural work, administration, etc.). Western governments must pay farmers a decent price for crop substitution. One policy option might be to accept that opium growing will continue while these countries remain poor and underdeveloped, and for Western governments to purchase opium at source for later destruction. The 3000kg of heroin that comes to Britain would cost between £600 000 and £3m to buy as opium from farmers (or between £9m and £12m from the wholesaler). A planned crop-intervention scheme would guarantee producers an income and interrupt supply at source. This is cheap compared with the estimated £200m a year that drug users in London alone spend on heroin – but costs would rise as more farmers began to cultivate opium for the market.

An alternative is to encourage development of a Third World

pharmaceutical industry based on locally grown drugs, legitimising controlled production, and furthering economic development.

What about importation and distribution? First, I suggest we should insist upon public accountability of resources and effectiveness. The 'value for money' calls now made on other state services are equally applicable to law enforcement. If there is a pay-off from the new resources which the present government is putting into law enforcement, we should expect over the next year to see some significant outcome in terms of several publicly available statistics – on number, quantity and size of drug seizures.

Second, what is the most effective and efficient means of law enforcement? At what levels should effort be expended? Is there a better return from more money for the police, or for the Customs? Certainly, the figures on drug seizures suggest a greater return from Customs' work: over 90 per cent of the total weight of heroin (and other drugs) is seized by Customs. Intercepting 1 kilo at import is clearly much cheaper than after it has been divided into 1000 separate 1-gram packets. There is need for more research on the effectiveness of the various Customs and police activities.

Third, there is the question of the relative allocation of resources to suppression of each of the drugs of misuse. Despite the emphasis in government policy on the problem of heroin and cocaine, cannabis continues to be a major target and accounts for the majority of drug seizures and convictions. If detection of all drugs requires similar efforts, then at present the majority of Customs and police resources are devoted to cannabis. What would be the impact of a redirection of resources from cannabis to heroin and cocaine?

Fourth, this debate must be informed by evidence of the impact of Customs and policing activity. Law enforcement has an impact not only on availability, but in shaping the distribution system, for example, the structure of drug markets, their location, and membership. Law enforcement is reasonably successful in keeping dealing off the streets (although the 'street' metaphor often used by agency workers and researchers can be misleading) and in keeping it confined to certain locations. We know little about the impact of policing. The rhetoric of police work (and a view shared by agency workers) is that control agencies should prioritise the pursuit of higher level dealers. We know this is a difficult task, even though it seems not to have been formally evaluated. Equally plausible might be a strategy that contains and limits dealing networks at a local level – also a hitherto unevaluated strategy. Here is an opportunity for law enforcement, agency workers and researchers to collaborate in local experiments in different enforcement strategies.

Finally, allocation of resources to law enforcement must be seen in the broader context of the total resources available to the drugs problem. Thatcher's optimism about the unlimited resources for the Custom's battle against smuggling – 'anything more we can do will be done and must be done' she is reported to have said – may make good press, but belies the complexity of the task. As I have argued, law enforcement alone is unlikely to have a major impact on the availability of drugs. Many will be asking for a broader consideration of the right balance between public expenditure on education, prevention and treatment, as well as enforcement. The money spent on the education and information campaigns, and on local treatment and rehabilitation projects while welcome, begins to look small in comparison with expenditure on enforcement.

Notes

1. For fuller discussions, and different analyses see Stimson and Oppenheimer, 1982; Berridge, 1984; Smart, 1984; Judson, 1973; Trebach, 1982.
2. Since 1968 Home Office statistics on addict notifications have been presented on a 'profit' and 'loss' table which start with those known at the beginning of the year (5079 in 1984), to which are added new notifications (7410), and from which are deducted those who for various reasons are removed from the tabulation during the year (for example, by reason of imprisonment or death or no longer 'seeking treatment') (6620). This gives a net figure of 5869. I think that a more realistic working figure is the gross number known at the year beginning, plus those notified during the year, a total of 12489. For discussion of problems in interpreting Home Office Statistics see Stimson, 1984.
3. Estimates from the Society of Civil and Public Servants (1985) show even more dramatic falls. They estimate the street price per gram of heroin as £250–350 in 1980, falling to £100–150 by 1983. These street prices are considerably higher than other estimates and have probably

been calculated on a basis different from that of other sources quoted. All sources agree there was an overall fall in price.

4. Any calculation of the total amount of heroin consumed in the United Kingdom is highly speculative. The estimated consumption of 3000kg in 1985 is based on the following assumptions. *Regular users*: 60 000 using a quarter gram per day of 45 per cent purity for four out of five days, gives a total of 1971kg per year pure heroin. *Casual users*: 120 000 using a quarter gram per week of 45 per cent purity, gives a total of 702kg per year pure heroin. Total amount of pure heroin is 2673kg, but assuming that on import this is in fact 90 per cent pure, the total amount at import is 2970kg. Another estimate, by J. A. Dellow, Assistant Commissioner at New Scotland Yard, suggests a national annual expenditure of £400m (*Guardian*, letter, 10 October 1986). This estimate takes the number of known addicts multiplied by 5, use for 7½ months a year, subtraction of 10 per cent for 'those acquiring but not purchasing', an average consumption figure, and known street prices. The actual figures in this equation are not given. If Dellow assumed average street price at £100 per gram, then £400m would buy 4000kg.

5. There are major problems for customs in controlling import of any goods. For example, there is a regular pattern of tobacco smuggling from Belgium to England. Journalists' interviews with importers indicate 1½ ton shipments three times a week, hidden inside containers of vegetables so that the overall lorry weight is consistent. It was estimated by one smuggler that only one load in fifty is seized (*Sunday Times*, 26 January 1986).

3

Social deprivation, unemployment and patterns of heroin use

Geoffrey Pearson

The problem of heroin misuse which has recently taken a new turn in some of Britain's run-down, working-class neighbourhoods and housing estates must be set alongside the burden of mass unemployment which lies upon so many of these same localities. It is as well to say at the outset that I do not mean by this that there is any necessary or mechanical relationship between unemployment and heroin use. This is obviously not true. If it were, then one would not find heroin being used in the social orbit of wealthy pop stars. Nor among those decadent upper reaches of 'Old England' where the young heirs and heiresses to multi-million pound fortunes, débutantes and Oxford undergraduates have apparently grown tired of only champagne for breakfast. Nor among young people in some of the more modestly affluent leafy suburbs whose heroin habits are sometimes nursed by their prosperous mothers and fathers.

Nevertheless, on all the available evidence there is undoubtedly an important and significant relationship between the problem of mass unemployment and Britain's new heroin problem, both of which have grown substantially since 1979 or thereabouts. The course which heroin takes in a person's life, or within their immediate community, will also differ significantly according to these other differences in opportunities and available resources. On this view, unemployment will make the effects of heroin more devastating, both for the individual user, his or her family, and the surrounding neighbourhood. The circumstances of unemployment will make it more likely that heroin misuse will spread more rapidly within a neighbourhood, once the drug has become available. Finally, the absence of a work status, with its rewards and commitments to compete with the claims of heroin, will make it more difficult for a user to relinquish the drug and its accompanying life-style.

It is often said that 'Heroin is the ideal drug for the unemployed'. But what exactly does that mean? My aim here will be to 'unpack' the various kinds of relationship between heroin use and unemployment which might (and indeed do) exist, and to show how these work on a number of different levels. I will draw partly on experience gained through research in the north of England during the spring and summer months of 1985 on behalf of the Health Education Council (cf. Pearson *et al.*, 1986), together with a variety of other research and writing both on drug misuse and the social and personal effects of unemployment. The assembled evidence suggests that it is futile to deny the links between unemployment and heroin. Equally, it would be wrong to suggest that these are anything but complex. The argument can neither be won nor lost by sticking to all-too-simple formulations such as whether or not unemployment 'causes' heroin misuse.

Some initial confusions and complexities

The relationship between heroin use and urban deprivation is not a new discovery, and it has been a matter of concern for many years in some North American cities such as Chicago and New York. In *The Road to H*, for example, a major study of heroin use among young delinquents in New York in the 1950s and early 1960s, it was found that the problem was not evenly distributed across the city. Rather, it was most densely concentrated in some of the city's worst slums, inhabited largely by Puerto Rican and black workers during the period of large-scale migration to New York, causing the authors of the study to speculate on whether a sense of futility and hopelessness in slum districts increased the likelihood that young people would experiment with narcotics (Chein *et al.*, 1964). In the years immediately following the Second World War, it had been in these same parts of New York that heroin misuse had first become prevalent. Heroin was cheap and plentiful, and between 1947 and 1951 it established itself as a social drug in use among adult migrant workers in these poor districts (Preble and Casey, 1969). The Chicago experience was somewhat different, however, in that the heroin epidemic which peaked around 1949 began initially on Chicago's negro south side with its swinging night-spots and the jazz scene among 'hip, street-wise, non-delinquents', and only from the early 1950s onwards did the heroin problem come to be increasingly identified with the lower-class delinquent 'dope fiend' (Hughes *et al.*, 1972).

One must be careful to distinguish, then, the initiating circumstances of a heroin epidemic from its subsequent development. Once established, however, the connections between heroin misuse and urban deprivation have been consistently noted in Chicago and New York through the 1960s and 1970s, and the densest concentration of heroin use and street-dealing in New York remains the poor ghetto districts of central and east Harlem (Johnson *et al.*, 1985; Hughes, 1977).

In Britain opiate use was, of course, virtually unknown throughout the 1940s and 1950s, although in London there were tiny gatherings of people around the West End jazz and 'bebop' clubs who were using heroin and other drugs (cf. Spear, 1969; MacInnes, 1985). During the 1960s, as patterns of drug use began to change, a large amount of concern focused on the use of 'pep pills' by young people and although heroin was undoubtedly becoming slowly more available its use was still nevertheless an extremely rare phenomenon in Britain. Indeed, even after the sharp increase in the number of heroin addicts known to the Home Office between the late 1960s and early 1970s there were no more than 3000 registered addicts (Stimson and Oppenheimer, 1982).

Until the early 1970s there had been no strong association between heroin use and any particular social group, although in relation to other drugs such as cannabis and LSD with the emergence of the 'hippie' life-style there was a strongly middle-class and student emphasis. With the exception of the use of various pills by working-class 'Mods' – 'bombers', 'blues' and 'purple hearts' – the British drug scene could still be largely summed up as 'Bohemian' in social orientation.

Through the 1970s the heroin problem in Britain largely

stabilised, with a tendency for the proportion of newly notified addicts under 21 years of age to drop steadily through these years (Hartnoll, 1984; Home Office, 1984). From the mid-1970s barbiturate misuse became increasingly common among younger drug users, although this caused surprisingly little social concern except among specialist professional groups, but as the 1970s wore on there was also a gathering together of a variety of social problems such as housing difficulties and unemployment in combination with problem drug use as youth unemployment began its slow creep upwards (Dorn and South, 1985; Jamieson *et al.*, 1984).

Sudden changes then overcame patterns of drug misuse in Britain, with the number of known addicts increasing threefold between 1979 and 1983 (Home Office, 1984). There was also a new style of drug use, of course, involving young people in some of the UK's battered working-class housing estates who began to experiment with the novel practice of smoking, 'chasing' or 'tooting' heroin. As this became popular from the early 1980s onwards, then for the first time in the history of heroin misuse in modern Britain there were clear associations between heroin and unemployment.

The watershed years were between 1979 and 1981, when from all the available evidence the heroin habit really began to take off in some of the towns and cities in Scotland and the north of England whereas previously it had been largely confined to London. Observable signs of a rapid increase in heroin use were first noted in Glasgow, for example, in 1981 (cf. Ditton and Speirits, 1981). Whereas in Bradford, to take one other example, heroin first became available in any quantity in 1979 at the absurdly low street-price of £35–40 a gram, compared with £80–£100 in London at that time. Such was the novelty of the situation in a city like Bradford that an out-reach drugs project reported that among experienced drug users, 'Most people felt that cheap heroin was just a flash in the pan' (Fox, 1979).

These were, of course, also the crucial years in which unemployment increased at an astonishing pace, doubling from approximately 1.5 million to 3 million people in the space of two years between 1979 and 1981. And as unemployment continued to increase through the 1980s, in spite of repeated attempts by the government to massage the figures by changing the basis on which the statistics were assembled, so the problem of heroin misuse continued to grow.

What, if any, were the associations between these twin phenomena of the early 1980s? At a macro-statistical level it has recently been shown that there is a close association between national trends of rising drug misuse and rising unemployment (Peck and Plant, 1986). Nevertheless, in my view it would be a mistake to infer from these statistical correlations that heroin misuse is directly caused by unemployment, or that the problem of heroin misuse can be blamed on those government policies which flowed from Margaret Thatcher's disastrous 'monetarist' experiment which has ripped the heart out of so many of our industrial towns and cities where heroin use is now so prevalent. The relationships between heroin use and unemployment are less direct than that. Indeed, at a national level they might even be described as 'accidental'. This is because the increase in heroin misuse was only made possible as a result of the influx of high-quality heroin in cheap and plentiful supply from the late 1970s onwards from Iran and Pakistan, so that the developments which made heroin more widely available at precisely the same time that domestic unemployment began to rise sharply were, at quite a vital level of argument, simply coincidental.

Even so, if the macro-correlations between levels of unemployment and heroin use might merely indicate an 'accidental' relationship between the two phenomena, evidence of a different kind is beginning to accumulate which shows an indisputable link between unemployment and heroin misuse at a local level. What I hope will also emerge from my subsequent argument is that high levels of unemployment make it much more difficult to build effective strategies in order to combat heroin misuse. This different kind of evidence, which shows that there is a tendency for heroin misuse to be concentrated in localities which are also suffering from high levels of unemployment, emerges both from our own research in the north of England and also that of Howard Parker and his colleagues on Merseyside (Parker *et al.*, 1986; Pearson *et al.*, 1986). And it is more focused, neighbourhood-based studies such as these which are beginning to throw up a number of difficult questions about the relationship between unemployment and heroin misuse which point in quite different directions from the blanket assumptions which underlie the kind of macro-statistical analysis which I have already mentioned.

Before trying to unravel these relations in more detail, it is first as well to emphasise once more that there is no mechanical relationship between heroin and unemployment, whereby unemployment leads inevitably towards an increased risk of heroin misuse. We know that heroin has sometimes spread like wildfire in depressed, run-down council estates in cities such as Glasgow, Manchester, Liverpool and elsewhere. Nevertheless, in some of the most socially deprived parts of the British Isles, such as Belfast and the north-east of England, heroin misuse is a rarity. Why? The simple answer is that the single necessary condition for the spread of drug misuse is an established distribution system – and without local availability heroin misuse, rather obviously, will not be found to be correlated with unemployment or any other social variable. And at the moment the extent to which heroin distribution systems have effectively penetrated the British Isles is extremely variable, so that one finds at the moment that the heroin problem is extremely scattered and localised. Thus, in some areas of high unemployment one does not find heroin misuse, whereas in others one does find dense pockets of the problem.

In the north of England, one aspect of this localisation is that there is less of a problem to the east of the Pennines than to the west. This is not to say that heroin misuse is unknown to the east of the Pennines – whether in the West Yorkshire conurbation of Bradford and Leeds, around Sheffield and Rotherham in South Yorkshire, the port of Hull, or some smaller and more remote towns. However, one does not find the highly visible and densely concentrated heroin networks which can be found to the west of the Pennines in some parts of Manchester and Merseyside, in a number of other towns in Lancashire and Cheshire, or in Carlisle towards the Scottish border. Moreover, where the availability of heroin is reduced in the east there is a tendency for its street-price to be that much higher than in the west. And in an area such as South Yorkshire it was agreed by all reliable sources during the summer of 1985 that something like 50 per cent of opiate use in the region consisted of illicit pharmaceuticals rather than imported heroin – which points once again to the weakness and inefficiency of the heroin distribution systems, as well as to previously established patterns and preferences of opiate misuse within the local drug culture (cf. Pearson *et al.*, 1986).

Substantial regional variations such as these can only really be understood in terms of distribution and supply mechanisms. We can identify even more detailed, fine-grained variations in drug availability at neighbourhood level whereby even in a town or city where there is an extensive heroin problem, the drug might be readily available in one neighbourhood but not in another. This was found in our research in the north of England, and also in Lee O'Bryan's recent research in London where he found that there might be a pattern of heroin use on one council estate, and yet the drug would not be available in an immediately adjacent neighbourhood (O'Bryan, 1985a).

In Parker's study on the Wirral, which involved a detailed and sophisticated calculation of prevalence rates for problem drug users, the prevalence of heroin use varied sharply between the different townships which constitute the region. These rates were correlated with a number of indicators of social deprivation including unemployment levels, showing a dominant tendency for high levels of heroin misuse to be associated with high levels of social deprivation. For a small number of townships these correlations did not hold; there was a serious heroin problem in some relatively affluent areas, and in one area of high social deprivation the level of drug misuse was low. However, the relatively prosperous areas with high levels of heroin misuse were found to be in close proximity to townships with high levels both of heroin misuse and unemployment, suggesting that in these areas geographical proximity had assisted the effective working of the local drug distribution networks, whereas the area of high deprivation with low drug misuse was geographically remote (Parker *et al.*, 1986). This particular finding from the Wirral study is especially valuable because it offers a compact illustration of how the spread of heroin misuse results from a number of interwoven factors. While the problem tends to be most densely concentrated in areas of high unemployment, it can also become a serious problem in a more 'affluent' locality if that locality has developed a distribution network. Nowhere is immune, but the social map still tends to indicate that social deprivation and heroin misuse are in some way linked.

We can begin to see in a preliminary way how the relationship between heroin and unemployment is not a simple, one-to-one connection. Rather, it is characterised by a high degree of local complexity. Even so, whatever the precise mechanism of these relationships, where heroin misuse has become a serious problem in recent years, those same neighbourhoods are likely to suffer from a number of other problems such as poor housing, low income, a high density of single-parent families, and unemployment. This is what needs to be explained.

The way in which I shall set about attempting to offer an explanation will be on three fronts. First, I will show why socially deprived neighbourhoods so often seem to provide a home for drug distribution networks. Second, drawing largely on North American experiences, I will examine some of the ways in which unemployment might act as an encouragement to experimentation with heroin. Third, I will discuss something of what is known about the social and personal consequences of unemployment, principally in terms of the social psychology of unemployment and how this might help us to understand why heroin misuse coheres with the life-style of the unemployed. Taken together, while these strands of evidence might not support the view that heroin is the 'ideal' drug for the unemployed, because in the long run it almost certainly exacerbates people's living difficulties rather than improves them, it will go some way to showing that the unemployed are 'ideal' for heroin.

Neighbourhood studies: unemployment, housing and heroin

One aim of our research in the north of England was to identify a small number of neighbourhoods where heroin misuse had become a serious problem, and to see whether these localities differed in any other significant ways from the surrounding area. For example, we were interested to learn whether these localities would show any identifiable pattern in terms of the age structure of their local population, the nature and standard of the housing stock, the proportion of single-parent families, or in terms of other 'social indicators' such as overcrowding, household access to a motor car and, of course, local unemployment levels.

On the basis of information from relevant public agencies

seven neighbourhoods were identified, although our independent enquiries subsequently established that two of these did not in fact have an extensive heroin problem – this was merely feared and rumoured by local people and by local professionals, who typically projected their anxieties onto housing estates that already had poor local reputations as 'problem estates'. It is probably fairly common that people tend to imagine that such 'problem areas' suffer from every conceivable kind of difficulty and it is often through such processes of negative stereotyping that such localities gain their local notoriety (cf. Reynolds, 1985; Gill, 1977). I will return to this question of local stereotyping at a later point.

For those neighbourhoods where a local heroin problem could be identified, a mass of detailed information was brought together from various public agencies such as housing departments, social services, the probation service, police and planning departments in order to understand the problems faced by residents in these areas. The Small Area Statistics of the 1981 Census proved quite invaluable, offering a measure of local conditions particularly well-suited to our purposes because heroin had started to become locally available in 1981 or thereabouts. Heroin users and ex-users were also contacted and interviewed in each of these localities, and extensive contacts were made with a variety of professional and voluntary bodies.

The chosen neighbourhoods varied in a number of respects. Of the original seven, two were medium-sized council estates built in the inter-war years and with poor local reputations, whereas two others were large post-war 'overspill' estates with a mixture of housing stock which included flats and maisonettes as well as conventional housing. Some were parts of large urban conurbations, while others were in smaller towns, and one of the chosen localities was a typically run-down high-rise development in an inner-city location. In all cases the large majority of the housing stock was publicly owned, and to all outward appearances these neighbourhoods were no different from innumerable other council estates dotted across the length and breadth of the north of England.

The thing which stood out, however, is that each of those neighbourhoods with a heroin problem was also experiencing unusually severe levels of social deprivation and unemployment.

In 1981 the national unemployment rate was approximately 12 per cent, but in these localities it varied from 23 per cent to 34 per cent, with even higher levels among young people under 25 years of age. On average, somewhat more than two-thirds of households did not have access to a motor car, and in some areas almost one-third of all households contained a single-parent family. These were, then, decidedly poor working-class neighbourhoods.

The Small Area Statistics of the Census enable us to take an even more locally focused view of the pattern of social deprivation in these neighbourhoods. The smallest unit of the census is the Enumeration District (ED) which will cover approximately 200 households in an urban area, and by using the ED statistics as 'building blocks' it is possible to generate a statistical profile not only of an overall housing area but also of particular sub-localities within the area, down to a small number of streets or a particular block of flats. When ED levels of the census are examined in this way they reveal dense pockets of exceptional poverty and social need (cf. Pearson, 1986). Social deprivation does not cast its shadow evenly across a single town or city, nor does it spread itself uniformly across even a single housing estate. Poverty and unemployment tend to dwell in small huddles of a few streets, and we were able to map these sharp local gradients for our identified neighbourhoods and to match these against 'target areas' where the local heroin network was at its highest density (see Table 3.1).

The results suggest a close local relationship between heroin misuse and neighbourhood levels of social deprivation and unemployment. For example, the 1981 unemployment level of 16 per cent in the north-west region rose to 23 per cent in one Merseyside town and to 34 per cent in its electoral Ward of Docktown. Then, in a locality defined by two Enumeration Districts (EDs) within the area, unemployment rocketed to 53 per cent with 60 per cent of young men under 25 years of age out of work. These two EDs described a high-rise development which was notorious for a variety of social problems, and which had now also become the home for an even more notorious heroin-dealing network. One ex-user from this neighbourhood described for us a typical daily scene in the corridors and stair-wells of this high-rise development:

Table 3.1 A neighbourhood analysis of 1981 census Small Area Statistics

	Unemployment* (%)	Unemployment under 25 years* (%)	One-parent families† (%)	No access to car (%)
Greater Manchester				
Moorside	24	28	31	69
Target area	33	45	31	72
Closefields	33	40	39	74
Target area	40	66	45	84
Greenleigh	23	30	29	62
Target area	36	46	34	73
Merseyside				
Docktown Ward	34	40	24	78
Target area	53	60	38	92
South Yorkshire				
Steelborough	29	35	30	65
Target area	44	47	36	74

* All unemployment rates refer only to male unemployment. Female unemployment statistics tend to underestimate the extent of unemployment because of non-registration.

† 'One-parent families' refers to the statistics in Table 31 of the 1981 Census. In Table 27 another estimate of single-parent households is offered which describes those households with children and one 'lone adult'. Table 27 gives a substantially lower estimate on all counts, but Table 31 is generally thought to offer the better estimate because it includes also single parents who might share a household with kin, other families or friends.

NOTE: Each named locality (Moorside, Closefields, etc.) refers either to a specific neighbourhood or electoral ward. Each 'Target area' refers to a sub-locality within that neighbourhood or ward where a specific heroin network was at its highest density. The statistical evidence, generated from the Enumeration District level of the Small Area Statistics of the 1981 Census, shows a gathering concentration of social deprivation within each Target area.

SOURCE: Pearson *et al.*, 1986.

You go in the area, like, and there's about . . . at the most about six people selling it there like, you know, it's like a market. You walk in, 'You're after gear?' 'Don't buy his gear, buy mine!' 'Here you are, mine's the best bags, here y'are look at these!' 'Fuck off, I've seen 'im first!' And all that, like. That's what it's like as you walk by. Like a big market stall.

This area had long been notorious because of structural and design problems which had led to damp in bedrooms and mould on the interior walls of the flats, as well as excessive heating bills for residents. Waste-disposal facilities had long since failed to operate properly and the area had entered that well-known spiral of decline whereby the majority of families were anxious to leave and only those with the most urgent and desperate housing needs were prepared to consider moving into the flats. It had become a 'hard-to-let' area, and as the proportion of empty and boarded-up household units increased, so the pressures on local residents increased. Also, significantly, the heroin problem began to take root.

The same spiral of disrepair was in evidence in the other localities, with particular streets or blocks of flats within the larger area suffering from the same 'hard-to-let' syndrome and with heroin misuse and its sustaining dealing networks tending to cluster within this smaller and more disadvantaged huddle of poverty. The ways in which multiple problems tend to gather together in this way in certain public housing estates has long been recognised, inviting a familiar controversy as to whether housing allocation policies which use certain estates (or small parts of them) as 'dumping grounds' for difficult tenants lie at the back of the downward spiral of morale and the concentrations of a variety of social problems (cf. Morris and Morris, 1955; NACRO, 1975; Gill, 1977; Reynolds, 1985; Coleman, 1985). It will invariably be denied by local housing departments that they operate such policies. But whether as a result of housing allocation policy or not, once a poor reputation is established this image will tend to be reinforced by selective news stories in the local press and by local gossip. As its 'hard-to-let' reputation intensifies, making it increasingly less likely that families will wish to move into the area, this leads to even more dense concentrations of residents with the most urgent housing difficulties. The likelihood of squatting will also increase, as the proportion of vacant dwellings and boarded-up properties increases, and for those residents unfortunate enough to live in what will by now have become an area of considerable notoriety there will be a variety of knock-on effects: such as the inability to obtain hire-purchase facilities or television rental once one's address is known to the relevant credit company.

In one area within our study, 'Moorside' in Greater Manchester, a local tenants' group complained bitterly about these kinds of difficulties. Indeed, one of the things which they most disliked and feared about the arrival of heroin in their neighbourhood was that it would simply bring about a further worsening of the estate's reputation. There was also a substantial elderly population on this estate, and a local general practitioner confided that the main impact which the heroin problem had had on his workload was not dealing with drug users, but the heightened fear and anxiety among elderly residents occasioned by local rumour and the possibilities of drug-related crime. 'Fear of crime' is, of course, something to which old people are particularly vulnerable (Maxfield, 1984).

There is an awful predictability about the ways in which the history of a 'problem estate' unfolds, as increasing numbers and varieties of difficulties crowd together. The same pattern emerges once again, with a number of points of local difference, in Frances Reynolds's study of the 'Omega' estate in the Midlands, summarised here by Alice Coleman (1985, p. 91):

> It gained its bad name from its initial associations, in 1957, with 'immigrant' workers from Wales, Scotland and Ireland and other parts of England, and also from the largely mistaken belief that slum-clearance tenants had been dumped there. Once labelled as a problem, the estate was unable to escape this image . . . its reputation is reinforced by exaggerated press reports of any incident associated with it. Some tenants say they are ashamed of giving their addresses, as they feel that the name of the estate disadvantages them in job applications or obtaining normal services. The estate has become the least popular in the city among people seeking council accommodation and, according to Reynolds, it is often the most desperate and disadvantaged people that accept dwellings there.

Having established, then, that there is nothing particularly unusual about those neighbourhoods which fell within our study of the heroin problem, we can take the argument one step further. Given the nature of housing markets, it does not require a declared housing allocation policy to produce the downward spiral of the 'hard-to-let' estate once this is set in motion. Rather, the very fact that it will only be those with the most desperate housing needs who will be prepared to move into such an area will itself further intensify its multi-problem character. Such people will include single-parent families, women and their families who have been subject to domestic violence and who are trying to place some distance between themselves and their violent spouses, together with the young homeless and others who command the least power and influence within the housing market. Equally, people with drug-related problems also tend to have a variety of social difficulties, including housing problems, so that they will be subject to precisely the same pressures of the housing market – a point argued forcibly by Dorn and South (1985) in their study of London 'street agencies' and the problems which their clientele face. The London drug scene, as they show, was profoundly influenced by the deterioration of the housing supply during the 1970s, with a particularly sharp squeeze in the private rented sector which had previously been a major resource for young people in London.

The dense clustering of social problems which we have found, including the association between local unemployment levels and heroin misuse, is therefore at least in part a consequence of the effects of the housing market and housing policies on poor and disadvantaged people. However, the fact that these market pressures bear upon problem drug users in much the same way that they do upon one-parent families does not only mean that one gets dense concentrations of different potential client groups within the same area. It also follows that the presence of problem drug users will increase the local availability of drugs. In the case of heroin, at the lowest level of the distributions chain we find those user-supplier or user-dealer networks in which roles are subject to change on a periodic basis: today it is this person who has a surplus who supplies to that person; tomorrow this person is short and secures his or her drugs from that person. 'User-dealers' or 'user-suppliers' are not just users who also happen to deal in order to support their habits. Drugs circulate at this lowest level essentially among friendship networks, within which there is a mutuality of interests and the roles of 'buyer' and 'supplier' are frequently interchanged. So that the presence of drug users in a locality makes it highly likely that the low-level dealing networks will establish themselves within the area. The easy availability of housing in 'hard-to-let' areas, together with the presence of unoccupied dwellings which invite squatting, thus act as major encouragements for the possibility that drug-dealing networks will emerge. Indeed, the most common form of user-dealer network that we encountered in our northern research was precisely someone doing business from the front room of his or her council house in a run-down area of a run-down estate. The open-market style of 'street dealing' mentioned earlier, which is reminiscent of North American 'copping areas', was in our experience highly exceptional – although there will often be neighbouring public houses and clubs where it is possible to 'score' drugs.

The complex pattern of ways in which social disadvantage works itself out within the confines of the housing market thereby have important consequences in terms of heroin's availability, with the increased likelihood that it will become more available at 'street level' in areas of high social disadvantage. Availability, as I have argued, is crucial to the dissemination of any pattern of drug use. But availability cannot in itself explain why people *choose* to use drugs. Availability can only lay the basis for the possibility of choosing to use a drug. And so the next question that we must ask is, what happens once heroin becomes available within a locality? And does unemployment play any part in the drug choices that people will make?

Activity or passivity? Messages from North America

The association between a high density of local heroin misuse and high levels of social and economic deprivation has been noted many times before, particularly in North American ghettos where there is a much more extensive and long-standing narcotics problem than in Britain. In attempting to account for these links, one dominant form of explanation has been to invoke the idea of heroin use as an 'escapist' or 'retreatist' activity: a flight into inactive phantasy in the face of a harsh world which promises little or nothing by way of material achievement.

This is a view which holds both a common-sense appeal, as well as drawing some authority from certain traditions within theoretical sociology and criminology. On the side of common sense, Pete Townshend of *The Who* has recently put it this way: 'I have often said, and many agree with me, that the high unemployment figures among young people in this country must be contributing to their growing use of oblivion-creating drugs' (quoted in Maden and Wallace, 1986). Whereas it was from the theoretical work of Robert Merton (1938 and 1957) that sociologists developed their own directly comparable 'escapist' theories of drug misuse. For Merton, while theft and property crime were to be viewed as 'innovative' means by which people delivered the promised goods of the American Dream through illicit acquisition, forms of deviance such as drug use or 'hobo' life-styles were grouped together as 'retreatist' adaptations by which people opted out of the challenges of the good life, neither attempting to earn the promised goods through honest toil nor aspiring to obtain them through illicit means.

Robert Merton's vast influence in North American sociology and criminology meant that this became a traditional line of thinking in the post-war years, subsequently reworked and reinforced by Cloward and Ohlin (1960) who understood involvement in drug cultures as a 'double failure' both in the world of licit and illicit acquisition. Delinquent subcultures, as they described them, could be divided on lines of specialisation. There were 'criminal' gangs in ghetto neighbourhoods in which there was opportunities for recruitment of young men into adult criminal activities, and where such gangs centred their activities on gainful theft and robbery. Then, in the absence of such opportunities, there were 'conflict' gangs whose preoccupations centred upon territorial gang fighting. But finally, for those young people in slum neighbourhoods who were involved in neither criminal gangs nor fighting gangs there were the 'retreatist' options of drug misuse.

In their study of delinquency and narcotics use in New York in the 1950s and early 1960s, *The Road to H*, Isidor Chein and his colleagues also adopted an 'escapist' perspective in trying to explain why there was a concentration of heroin misuse in areas of urban deprivation. It was suggested that young people in such neighbourhoods were more likely to experiment with narcotics because the 'conditions of economic squalor may generate a sense of hopelessness from which narcotics offer at least a temporary, if illusory, escape' (Chein *et al.*, 1964, p. 78).

However, this view of drug misuse as a passive, escapist activity subsequently came to be challenged by a significant body of research within North American criminology, much of it concerned with the Chicago and New York heroin epidemics of the late 1940s and 1950s. A more active view of the heroin user's life-style was developed, both in terms of the pursuit of pleasure and status, by Finestone (1957) and Hughes *et al.* (1972) who described in similar terms how the Chicago heroin epidemic which peaked in 1949 had been associated with the 'cool' life-style adopted by young black 'cats' in the context of the emerging modern jazz culture of Chicago's black south side. The penalties for heroin possession were not severe at this time, and much less severe than penalties for marijuana possession, and as Hughes *et al.* (1972, p. 995) describe them, 'young addicts of the 1940s were hip, street-wise, non-delinquents'.

From San Francisco, Sutter (1966) also failed to support the idea of a passive and retreatist drug subculture, describing instead an elaborate status system within which the supreme status was afforded to the 'righteous dope fiend' – the successful addict rarely seen in either hospitals or clinics, who could even be something of a local hero. Feldman's (1968) research, based on fieldwork in Boston and New York, offered further credibility to the view of an active addict-life-style with its detailed accounts of how narcotics served as a means by which 'action-seeking' youth in slum neighbourhoods could demonstrate their claims to manhood and also claim status as a 'stand-up cat'. And then at more or less the same time, undoubtedly the most explicit departure from the 'passive', 'retreatist' view of heroin use was offered by Preble and Casey (1969) from New York, where the street-addict was described as a resourceful entrepreneur, engaged in a flurry of economic activity which required him to remain 'alert, flexible and resourceful' in order to 'take care of business' successfully.

In Feldman's account of the world of 'action-seeking' slum

youth, status as a 'stand-up cat' had been commonly achieved through being adept at thieving and fighting, thereby facing and overcoming various challenges to one's emerging manhood. However, heroin came to be a most effective form of challenge precisely because of its fatal notoriety. Whether the 'stand-up cat' was prepared to accept the challenge, and whether he would then be able to use the drug without succumbing to addition and dependence, could become a crucial test of manhood in some poor districts. 'Are you man enough to take it?' 'Can you control it, or will it control you?' These were a much more mortal form of combat than a street-fight. Indeed, Feldman went on to suggest that once the challenge had been accepted then the experience of heroin might itself transform what it meant to be a true 'stand-up cat'.

Where the stand-up cat was admired for his bursts of hot hate, the new image ideal is admired for his coolness. Instead of brutality and physical strength, the new drug user prefers to be seen as slick and clever. Fighting becomes an unprofitable choice of behaviour, unless it involves access to drugs . . . He starts to lose his belief that walking away from a fight will make him a 'punk' or a 'faggot' . . . He simply believes, finally, that fighting is silly, very uncool especially when his 'high' can be achieved – so he thinks at this stage of his career – with far less risk to life and limb (Feldman, 1968, p. 137).

Preble and Casey described a similar transformation of the delinquent life-style in New York during the 1950s, as heroin became increasingly available, involving once more a shift from the 'tough' fighting image to the 'cool' and resourceful drug-user image:

The more street-wise teenagers learned about it and prevailed upon the experienced users to introduce them to it. Contrary to popular reports, experimentation with heroin by youths usually began at their initiative, and not through proselytism. The stereotype of the dope *pusher* giving out free samples of narcotics to teenagers in school yards and candy stores in order to addict them is one of the most misleading myths about drug use. Also, contrary to professional reports about this development, it was not the weak, withdrawn, unadaptive street boy who first started using heroin, but rather the tough, sophisticated and respected boy, typically a street gang leader . . . By 1955 heroin use among teenagers on the street had become widespread, resulting, among other things, in the dissolution of fighting gangs. Now the hip boy on the street was not the swaggering, leather-jacketed gang member, but the boy nodding on the street corner enjoying his heroin high. He was the new hero model (Preble and Casey, 1969, p. 6).

The likelihood that it would be opinion-leaders within neighbourhoods and friendship networks who were the first to experiment with heroin was also noted by Patrick Hughes and his colleagues in Chicago, again showing how status enhancement and attempts to emulate people with high local status is a powerful motor in the local dissemination of heroin habits (Hughes *et al.*, 1971 and 1972; Hughes and Crawford, 1972; Hughes, 1977). Their case studies of local drug epidemics adopted an approach which drew explicitly on earlier critiques of drug misuse as a 'retreatist' activity, and showed vividly how rapidly heroin can move within a friendship network. The notion of the 'pusher', again, was seen to be an irrelevance in understanding local drug networks. Indeed, as one begins to grasp the centrality of friendship and systems of local loyalty in shaping drug choices and preferences of life-style, a number of the stereotypical views of heroin use can be seen to be not only irrelevant but positively harmful. If it were not for the fact that friendship is the essential lubricant of drug exchanges, for example, then it is unlikely that heroin would be able to establish itself so quickly in a neighbourhood once it becomes available: the fact of friendship makes it more likely that the initial offer will be accepted than if it were offered by a stranger or a 'pusher' (cf. Pearson *et al.*, 1986; Pearson, 1987a; Bennett and Wright, 1986; Moore, 1977). The central drift of this argument is also that it makes little sense to think of heroin use as 'escape':

The user turns to drugs, not as a result of anomie, but rather to capitalise on a new mode of enhancing his status and prestige within a social system where the highest prizes go to persons who demonstrate attributes of toughness, daring and adventure.

Within the life-style of the stand-up cat, movement into heroin use is one route to becoming 'somebody' in the eyes of the important people who comprise the slum network (Feldman, 1968, p. 138).

These North American responses to the heroin epidemics of the late 1940s, 1950s and 1960s suggest a quite different interpretation of the links between heroin misuse and social deprivation than that which assumes that heroin is the 'ideal' drug of the unemployed because it promises oblivion. Rather, it is more helpful to think of drug misuse as offering a means of status-achievement to people who live in working-class neighbourhoods where they are deprived of the traditional means of demonstrating status through work.

This view is given further support by more recent British and North American research which suggests that it is not only more fruitful to think of the development of heroin networks in terms of what they contribute to local status systems, but also to the local economy (cf. Auld *et al.*, 1984 and 1986; Johnson *et al.*, 1985). John Auld and his colleagues have suggested, for example, that within the flourishing system of perks, fiddles and minor thefts which constitutes the so-called 'irregular economy' or 'hidden economy' in so many localities, heroin simply becomes one more commodity with an exchange value. It also offers – as they acknowledge from the work of Preble and Casey – the possibilities of an exciting and exacting life-style. Indeed, the importance of these insights from New York in the late 1960s has now been amply demonstrated by the major research into heroin-abuse crime in central and east Harlem (Johnson *et al.*, 1985) which shows how even at its lowest levels of street distribution, drug networks involve a myriad of exchange values both in terms of drug-dealing and drug-related crime. In a detailed fleshing-out of the Preble and Casey thesis, the street addict emerges as someone who is engaged in prolific economic activity, albeit within an illicit economy, with an average yearly cash-flow for the Harlem street-user of approximately $25 000 per year. Perhaps the most astonishing thing to come through in this research, however, is what the authors describe as the 'jarring realisation' that 'from a purely economic standpoint, heroin-abuser criminality is not all bad. In fact, although crime victims sustain important economic losses (not to mention non-economic considerations such as fear of crime, anger, frustration), more persons gain than lose' (Johnson *et al.*, 1985, p. 184). This comes about because of the way in which stolen goods are offered for sale at only a small proportion of their normal price, thus enlarging the purchasing power of poor families and helping to sustain the 'vigorous demand for stolen goods in ghetto economies':

> Moreover, our heroin abuser's theft had indirect effects on society by increasing monetary wealth in the licit economy. Victims bought replacements for the stolen goods, stores transferred shoplifting losses to consumers, and the government gained added sales-tax revenue. The licit economic system indirectly gained about $6,000 in additional economic values that would not have been realised had the heroin abuser not stolen merchandise . . . We are not claiming that heroin-abuser theft is good for the economy or society, only that many individuals benefit while fewer have specific, definable losses (Johnson *et al.*, 1985, pp. 184–5).

By comparison with New York the heroin scene in Britain is in its infancy, although it should not be imagined that the extraordinary economic scenarios drafted by Bruce Johnson and his colleagues are entirely irrelevant to the British experience and refer only to the wilder side of Harlem street life. The British heroin market, as described most recently by Lewis *et al.* (1985) is not yet characterised by the extraordinary division of labour described in Harlem, with its legion of different roles in the low-level distribution system – 'street dealers', 'jugglers', 'lieutenants', 'drop-men', 'steerers', 'taste faces' and 'bag followers' (cf. Preble and Casey, 1969; Johnson *et al.*, 1985; Rosenbaum, 1981). Even so, the economic consequences of an established heroin network within a locality can be quite considerable. Here is an ex-user from a deprived area of Merseyside, for example, describing how user-dealers that he had known operated in his neighbourhood:

> They'll buy a gram, which'll cost 'em from £60 to £75. Now what they'll do is cut £70 worth, say, into £5 or £10 bags. The rest of what's left of the gram is their smoke for the day. They go sell that £70 worth of gear . . . well, that's enough for the

next gram. And so on. You see, not making any money, but just supplying their habit sort of thing . . . Doing that, you know, from day to day like.

This is undoubtedly one of the lowest levels of a heroin distribution network, describing the 'typical' activity of a user-dealer or user-supplier through which no surplus profits are made, and where the aim is simply to supply one's own habit. Viewed in one light it is simply a hand-to-mouth 'subsistence' economy. If this activity is viewed economically from a cash-flow viewpoint, however, then it takes on a rather different complexion – whereby if this person were able to sustain his £70 daily transaction for a full year, it would represent an annual cash flow of £25 000. It would still be true that he would not be making any cash profit out of this low-level business, and would remain as poor as a church mouse. Nevertheless, it takes little imagination to see that in a socially deprived area with high unemployment levels, an annual cash flow of £25 000 is a phenomenal achievement. With something like £500 per week passing through his pockets, such a young man would be likely to be a figure of some real local standing. There would always be a little spare cash around. He would be the man to know if you wanted to score a 'bag' (of heroin), because even if he did not have any heroin immediately available he would possess a sound working knowledge of the local scene. Indeed, whether you prefer to think of him as a 'resourceful entrepreneur' in Bruce Johnson's terms or as an abject victim of the heroin traffic, locally he would undoubtedly be 'Jack the Lad'.

Life on the dole: killing time and creating meaning

Having seen how the North American experience suggests that it is not helpful to think of experimentation with heroin as an 'escapist' activity, I now wish to suggest that heroin use can nevertheless offer a sort of 'solution' to some of the problems experienced by people who are unemployed. The pharmacology of opiates, for example, is often described as one which offers a 'cushioning' effect against the world, and which 'takes all your worries away'. But once a pattern of addictive heroin use has been established, the user's life begins to circle around the overriding preoccupation of avoiding withdrawal symptoms. And this new worry, of supporting a 'habit', insists on an extremely active life-style – thereby dictating an aim and purpose in life, helping to cement the relationships between heroin misuse and those people whose lives have become aimless through unemployment.

In order to explore these new dimensions of the relationships between heroin use and unemployment, however, it will be helpful to forget about heroin for a moment and to focus on the lives of the unemployed. People, that is, who are *not* using heroin, and who are not involved in any other kinds of serious drug misuse, but who find themselves without work and without the prospect of paid employment in any foreseeable future. What is life like on the dole?

A great deal of rhetoric by politicians repeatedly suggests that unless something is done about mass unemployment, and in particular youth unemployment, then there will be more inner-city riots, more youthful hooliganism, more vandalism, and so on. Maybe this is true. Although the more obvious fact about the actual lives and experiences of the unemployed is not that unemployment produces restlessness and riot, but that it leads to apathy and despair. This was the experience of the 'Great Slump' of the 1930s, just as it is today. Which is not to say that there were not serious riots among the unemployed in Britain in the 1920s and 1930s, because there were – then as now (cf. Pearson, 1983 and 1987b). Even so, a typical 'day in the life' of an unemployed person in Britain today will be characterised more by a listless apathy than by revolt. Unemployment defines people as worthless and robs them of vital props to status and self-esteem. The ways in which identity is bound up with the job which someone does are many-sided, and this is particularly so among the male working-class where the skills of a bricklayer, the manly strength of a labourer, the resourcefulness of a car mechanic, are highly-prized social attributes. This is not to say that unemployment does not have its own demoralising effects on women. We know from Brown and Harris's 1978 study *The Social Origins of Depression* that a lack of employment outside the home was one of the factors which made it more likely that a woman would suffer from depression. But we actually know far much less about the specific effects of unemployment on women, just as we know much less about the lives and drug careers of female heroin users (cf. Griffin, 1985; Rosenbaum, 1981).

Policy discussions on unemployment often focus only on material and financial considerations, and although these are not unimportant a variety of social and personal consequences flow from what we can usefully think of as the social psychology of unemployment (cf. Jahoda, 1982; Jahoda *et al.*, 1938; Zawadski and Lazarsfeld, 1935; Pearson, 1987c). I have already touched upon the loss of status and identity, and people also lose a range of social contacts which come through their engagement with the workplace. Correspondingly, there is a tendency to lose interest more generally in external affairs. In one of the classic studies of the 1930s, Marie Jahoda's analysis of the impact of the Slump on the Austrian cotton town of Marienthal, it was found that unemployment had a surprisingly wide variety of knock-on effects. It resulted, for example, in a sharp decrease in the likelihood that someone would read a newspaper or use a library, even though these were facilities being made available to the unemployed at reduced cost, and there was a corresponding decline in other involvements with the external world such as political organisations and clubs. Diet and health were also subsequently affected, and a large body of evidence now indicates a clear relationship between unemployment and a variety of physical and mental ill health, as well as the increased likelihood of suicide (cf. Hakim, 1982). A more subtle effect which emerged with particular clarity in the Marienthal study, however, was the impact which unemployment had on the experience of the passage of time, in that unemployment seemed to have the effect of destroying the habitual time structures by which we order so much of our everyday life (Jahoda *et al.*, 1938).

Those of us fortunate enough to be in work will often curse these same time-structures – the need to get up every morning at the same time, to catch the same bus or train, to clock in and clock out at certain hours, to work to the strict timetable of the factory or the office, and so on – which are experienced as a burden and a strain. And so they are. But if these routine time-structures are suddenly removed, through unemployment or retirement, then people are often left feeling bewildered and rudderless. One of the findings of the Marienthal study was that everything seemed to take twice as long for unemployed men as it did when they were in work. It was observed that people even walked at a measurably slower pace in the streets. And yet, equally, although these men had so much time on their hands they seemed quite unable to meet deadlines effectively, and their wives would complain that they seemed unable to turn up punctually at meal times. It was as if without a routine time-structure which broke up the day, time and the passage of time became quite meaningless.

This is not, of course, some kind of 'natural' phenomenon. Rather, it is an aspect of our culture in which since the urban and industrial revolutions of the eighteenth and nineteenth centuries time has become dominated by the requirements of factory and office routines and time-clocked work (cf. Thompson, 1967; Simmel, 1950; Reid, 1976). Whereas in the pre-industrial world the most significant passages of time were those dictated by the seasons (sowing and harvesting) and the natural rhythms of the sun, moon and tides, we have now become so accustomed and socialised into our own habitual time-structures that these present themselves to us as if they were 'natural' and we find it difficult to cope without them. Marie Jahoda suggests that the unemployed are required to carry a 'heavy psychological burden' resulting from 'the destruction of a culturally imposed time-structure'. Moreover, 'to blame the unemployed for their inability to use their time in a more satisfactory way . . . would amount to asking that they single-handedly overthrow the compelling social norms under which we all live and which provide a supportive frame within which individuals shape their individual lives' (Jahoda 1982, p. 23).

The experience of the dislocation of routine time-structures will undoubtedly differ for people who have been in different kinds of employment, from different social classes, and also between men and women. Among other important occupational and regional variations revealed by detailed study of daily routines of activity and time-allocation, gender differences are undoubtedly central (cf. Parkes and Wallis, 1978; pp. 83–7). For women engaged in full-time work as housewives and child-carers, for example, we might expect that they would be less affected by the removal of time-structures imposed by external employment – and this was the experience in Marienthal. Within the busy round of shopping, cooking and cleaning there are some fixed landmarks within domestic labour (getting the children up, getting them off to school, preparing an evening meal, bed-time, etc.) but time is relatively unstructured. There is nothing to say that dishes should be washed before shopping, or that beds should be made before visiting the launderette, etc. Even so, the fact that many women will devise quite rigid timetables by which to order the day reminds us of how important it can be to have one's day guided and informed by supporting time-structures. One less obvious way of building some structure into a woman's day is suggested by Hilary Graham's (1976) study of smoking during pregnancy, whereby smoking a cigarette can become a means of marking out time to oneself − 'getting your feet up' − amidst an otherwise demanding round of household and child-care responsibilities.

What I now wish to suggest is that heroin use within the contexts of unemployment can take on a new significance, as an effective resolution of the problem of de-routinised time-structures. Dependence on heroin, quite literally, imposes its own rigid time-structure involving a necessary cycle of events if withdrawal sickness is to be avoided. In his formal ethnography of heroin use, *Ripping and Running*, Michael Agar describes the formal sequence of events necessary in order to sustain a successful heroin habit in terms of the 'central events in the life of a street junkie':

> The three were *hustle* (obtain money illegally), *cop* (buy heroin) and *get off* (inject heroin) . . . A junkie *hustles* to get *bread* (money); he cops to obtain *stuff* (heroin); and he *gets-off* to get *straight* (not-sick) . . . The outcome of *hustling* is *bread*, which is a prerequisite for *copping*. The outcome of *copping* is *stuff*, which is a prerequisite for *getting-off*. The outcome of *getting-off* is to be *straight*, which is a prerequisite for *hustling*. The three events are logically linked together between the outcome of one and the prerequisite of another (Agar, 1973; p. 21).

This same cycle of events was described to us repeatedly, albeit in less formal language, in interviews with heroin users and ex-users in northern cities. The rhythm of a heroin user's day was often described as if it were dictated by the beat of a metronome, of getting up, hustling for money, buying heroin, smoking it, and then hustling for the next bag:

> Like you get up, you've gotta go out, get your money, get your smack, come back, use it . . . You're alright for ten minutes, go back out again, get money . . . you're turkeying after a couple of hours, can't get nothin', whatever, back out again . . . (Colin, 23 years, Manchester).

'What was your typical day like?'

> Yeh just get your gear, smoke it, and then . . . wonder where you'll get your next bag from and watch a bit of telly, well that's it . . . that just makes you realise and you start thinking 'God, what am I gonna do for tonight now?' . . . So, like, you try and go and get more money, and that like, so your whole day's just taken up . . . Go and do whatever you do for your money, buy your gear, get back, by then like . . . you smoke it . . . then tea-time comes around (Sharon, 21 years, Merseyside).

> When I, when you're hooked on it like, you don't want to go robbin' until you had a toot like, 'cos you can't run or nothin' if you got grabbed by the busies [police]. You wouldn't be able to leg away, and that, like. So you'd have a toot to get your head together and then go out mooching (Eddie, 21 years, Merseyside).

These busy cycles of activity were commonly experienced as all-consuming preoccupations. So much so that if and when someone attempted to 'come off' and 'stay off' heroin, the question of how to break from the routine and replace it with a new and different pattern of daily activity could be experienced as a more difficult obstacle to overcome than actually withdrawing from heroin. In common with many other accounts of ex-users, 'coming off' was seen as relatively easy compared with 'staying off', and it was sometimes felt that the problem of 'staying off' was made all that more difficult by the absence of employment possibilities which would be able to supply both alternative routines and rewards:

It just seems the hardest thing in the world to stay off smack
. . . like I say, I've been off it a week, more than a week, but
you go back on it 'cos it's round here, you know . . . I think,
like, unemployment and that has got to do with it . . . with
nothing to do, I'm sitting here, like, doing nothing . . . I'm not
trying to blame anyone else like, but I'm bound to start
thinking of smack again (Jack, 22 years, Merseyside).

Getting out of the little rut you've been in for the last, y'know,
12 or 16 months or whatever . . . You know, getting up in the
morning, going down for your gear, or getting up and finding
some money to get your gear . . . smoking the gear, what have
you . . . It's just the actual boredom, you know, sitting in the
house . . . Like when I do come off, I just stay in the house
. . . just hibernate sort of thing . . . just stay in and become a
fucking hermit and that (Paul, 24 years, Merseyside).

It takes time, 'cos for two-and-a-half years like, all you've been
interested in is getting a bag . . . getting a bag . . . and you get
used to that. That's a routine for you like. So . . . (Eddie, 21
years, Merseyside).

On the one hand, these daily routines of a heroin habit can be
seen as a dismal compulsion from which the user cannot escape.
But at the same time they offered to people meaningful structures
around which to organise their lives in an eventful and challenging
way. In the absence of competing routines and structures of
meaning and identity, such as might be supplied by work
commitments, we can then say that it will not only be more
difficult to 'come off' and 'stay off' heroin by breaking out of its
routines and replacing them with alternative patterns of daily
activity. It will also be more likely that a novice user will establish
a pattern of habitual heroin use in the first place. Heroin is not
instantly addictive, and it is necessary to work quite hard at
becoming a heroin addict: that is to say, the drug will need to
have been taken regularly on a daily basis for some length of time
before the onset of dependence. Different time-scales are
undoubtedly involved for different individuals in making the
transition from early experimentation and occasional use to
habitual use, but it seems highly likely that this transition will be

accelerated where there are no competing claims on the user's time and attention, such as the possibilities of work commitments. And saying this is to imply more than that 'the devil makes work for idle hands'. Rather, it is an issue that bears very directly on what is known of the conditions necessary to sustain a pattern of occasional heroin use on an experimental, recreational basis for any length of time.

The question of occasional heroin use is little understood in contemporary Britain, but in North America where occasional opiate use on a recreational basis is known within the drug culture as 'chipping', research by Norman Zinberg and his colleagues has established some of the ground-rules which enable people to sustain non-addictive patterns of opiate use over long periods of time (cf. Zinberg, 1984). Basically, it is necessary for the occasional user to adhere to strict rules on the frequency of use, so that the drug is only used on certain occasions and never on consecutive days, which itself implies access to a knowledgeable network of controlled drug users who can offer advice to the novice. Zinberg's research also shows that non-compulsive heroin use is more easily sustained where there are other valued commitments in a person's life such as employment, family responsibilities and recreational pursuits which conflict with regular opiate use, together with a circle of friendship which includes non-users as well as users.

Other research confirms this general impression that occasional intoxicant use is more easily sustained, without leading to compulsive use, where there are competing claims in a person's life. Stanton Peele, for example, takes the view that the social–psychological basis of addictive experiences is more important than their physiological components, suggesting that people become addicted to experiences and not to substances. Compulsive behaviour, he points out, is commonly associated with practices such as gambling, food intake, or even the pursuit of physical fitness. What distinguishes controlled opiate users from compulsive users, on this view, is that they 'subordinate their desire for a drug to other values, activities and personal relationships, so that the narcotic or other drug does not dominate their lives. When engaged in other pursuits that they value, these users do not crave the drug or manifest withdrawal on discontinuing their drug use' (Peele, 1985, p. 8).

In Britain a smaller study by Blackwell (1984) identified similar features in the life-styles of controlled opiate users, while also noting the way in which people often moved between different statuses of involvement with heroin. Occasional users sometimes felt that their heroin use was drifting out of control towards dependence, whereupon they took action to regulate their involvement with the drug. Among the motivating factors mentioned in this context were 'loss of appetite, irregular sleep patterns, needle marks and spotty complexions', whereas 'two respondents said that they stopped using in order to get into shape for the football season' (Blackwell, 1984, p. 228). What is remarkable about these accounts is that, given the common view of heroin as a totally enslaving preoccupation, such trite reasons as 'getting into shape for the football season' could provide sufficient incentive to become abstinent.

The overall impression created by this body of research on controlled opiate use is that if occasional use is to be sustained over time, then there must be other commitments in a person's life which compete with the claims of heroin. If such commitments are either absent or not valued, then the work of Zinberg, Peele and others would suggest that stable patterns of recreational heroin use would not be commonly found within a drug-using community. Thus in an area of mass unemployment, one might expect that heroin misuse would quickly assume a pattern of epidemic growth once it becomes available in a locality simply because of the absence of any realistic promise of work commitments which provide a major means by which people in our culture fashion self-esteem and a meaningful identity. Indeed, when asked why she thought that some people seemed to be able to use heroin occasionally without becoming dependent whereas other people did not, the mother of an ex-user from an area of high unemployment in South Yorkshire offered an admirable impromptu version of the Zinberg–Peele thesis in the following terms:

Don't you think you've got to put it this way? People what are working, if they've got good sense, they've got sommat good to look out for. They're not gonna tek it, are they, through t'week when they're going to work. Whereas you get somebody what's in't unemployed, they'll have it at weekend and they'll continue wi' it, cos they got nowt else to do have they? Because you do get sensible people like that, don't you, if they're working they just . . . they'll not bother wi' it through t'week. Well that's how I see it.

And that, basically, is how I see it too. The relationships between heroin use and unemployment work on a number of levels. First, the gathering together of a potential for heroin misuse in areas of high social deprivation is determined by the mechanism of the housing market which brings together people with only the most urgent housing needs, including problem drug users, in run-down 'hard-to-let' areas of our towns and cities. By this means heroin can become available within a locality, with the potential that the drug comes to be used within a local friendship network on an experimental basis. A major encouragement to such experimentation is that in the absence of other effective means by which to establish meaningful lives and identities in areas of mass unemployment, a willingness to face the challenge of heroin can become a means by which to achieve local status, with every indication that the first people to use the drug within a locality will be opinion-leaders. The promise of small monetary gain, or at least the status of being someone 'in the know', further enhances the likelihood of heroin involvement as the drug establishes itself as one of a variety of commodities in circulation within the local hidden or irregular economy. In the absence of any other sustaining life commitments within such a neighbourhood it is then all the more likely that patterns of occasional use will pass over into habitual use more quickly than they would under different circumstances. Finally, the life-style of the heroin user with its necessary and exacting daily routines can not only appear to 'solve' what Marie Jahoda has called 'the heavy psychological burden' of unemployment caused by the dislocation of habitual time-structures, but the conditions of mass unemployment make it all the more difficult for heroin users to quit these routines and to establish alternative patterns of daily activity that are both meaningful and rewarding.

Once such a position has been arrived at, and by the mid-1980s it had already begun to arrive in some of the deprived neighbourhoods of British towns and cities, it then requires one final grim step to acknowledge that the situation in the ghetto districts of New York in the late 1960s, described by Edward Preble and John Casey, has become almost an adequate description of heroin misuse in unemployed Britain today. Noting the dominant tendency to view heroin use as 'an escape from life', theirs was an utterly explicit rejection of such a viewpoint. Indeed, in the ghetto contexts of economic and social disadvantage, they were more inclined to see the heroin user's hectic activity as a form of work:

> Their behaviour is anything but an escape from life. They are actively engaged in meaningful activities and relationships seven days a week. The brief moments of euphoria after each administration of a small amount of heroin constitute a small fraction of their daily lives. The rest of the time they are aggressively pursuing a career that is exacting, challenging, adventurous and rewarding. They are always on the move and must be alert, flexible and resourceful. The surest way to identify heroin users in slum neighbourhoods is to observe the way people walk. The heroin user walks with a fast, purposeful stride, as if he is late for an important appointment – indeed, he is. He is hustling . . . trying to sell stolen goods, avoiding the police, looking for a heroin dealer with a good bag . . . coming back from copping . . . looking for a safe place to take the drug, or looking for someone who beat [cheated] him – among other things. He is, in short, *taking care of business*, a phrase which is so common with heroin users that they use it in response to words of greeting, such as 'how you doing?' and 'what's happening?' *Taking care of biz* is the common abbreviation. *Ripping and running* is an older phrase which also refers to their busy lives. For them, if not for their middle- and upper-class counterparts (a small minority of opiate addicts), the quest for heroin is the quest for a meaningful life, not an escape from life. And the meaning does not lie, primarily, in the effects of the drug on their minds and their bodies; it lies in the gratification of accomplishing a series of challenging, exciting tasks, every day of the week (Preble and Casey, 1969, pp. 2–3).

To be realistic, policy proposals in relation to heroin should take into account the ways in which those people who live in deprived areas have evolved a variety of ways of getting by, including illicit economic activity and leisure activities, that fit the material conditions in which they live. Economic policies have a bearing here. While government policy may not have directly caused the heroin problem, a policy which tolerates scandalously high levels of unemployment makes it much more difficult to solve. Indeed, I think it highly unlikely that it will prove possible to contain the spread of heroin misuse, let alone curb it, until policies are adopted which offer to young working-class people realistic opportunities to obtain effective financial rewards and to fashion meaningful identities and life-styles through work and access to decent housing.

4

How families and communities respond to heroin

Martin Donoghoe, Nicholas Dorn, Christine James,
Stephen Jones, Jane Ribbens and Nigel South

How people respond to heroin at local level is of interest to all those concerned with the relationship between social policy and social action. First, from the point of view of social policy, drug problems generally and heroin-related problems specifically are seen as one arena in which policies of community care, self-help and parental responsibility are being tested out. Are such policies feasible, are they desirable, and how do they work in practice?

Second, from the broader point of view of an interest in how individuals and social groups first construct and then negotiate crises, the responses of family members and others at local level give us a rare glimpse of a private world of fears, guilt, horrors and personal struggles that only occasionally become publicly visible. This is the level of experience to which social policy ought to be attentive but all too often is not. Our interest in looking at this area is not a form of voyeurism, but an interest in the relationship between 'personal troubles' and 'public issues' (C. Wright Mills, 1970, p. 14).

Our material is drawn from two complementary studies carried out by researchers at the Institute for the Study of Drug Dependence. Both studies reflect concerns peculiar to the time. One was concerned with the question of how family members (generally parents, and most commonly mothers) respond to their relatives' (generally their sons', less frequently their daughters') heroin use.[1] From a social policy point of view, this study resonates closely with current concerns with 'parental responsibility', whilst from a social science perspective it picks up themes around the family, sexual divisions and mothering that are increasingly receiving the attention previously denied them in the post-war years. The second study was concerned with the question of how a variety of persons at local or neighbourhood level, including not only parents of users but other residents, voluntary workers and professionals, perceive the beginning of heroin problems in their localities – if indeed they do perceive such problems in their early stages.[2]

Taken together, the two studies give us a unique data set, covering private and public responses to heroin use. The presentation given here is of necessity very much an overview; we restrict ourselves to certain selected themes, and do not go into detail. Our purpose is to bring out some basic points, which we summarise here:

1. *Disaster planning*   As with other social and health problems, it is difficult to identify realistic preventive tasks and preparations for coping *before* the problem manifests itself. Preparations can be attempted in advance of the problem, but enthusiasm, momentum and indeed funding may quickly flag as people tire of hearing the cry 'wolf!'. Furthermore, in the absence of direct experience of responding to a problem locally, heightened levels of expectation may lead to unhelpful speculation and misinformation about the nature of drug problems. Lay people, professionals and police, for example, may develop quite strange expectations, as our initial case study shows. Other members of the community, including the majority of parents, seem to 'switch off'. Until there really *is* an expansion of drug use locally, there may be little that can be done in the way of practical preparations. And if there is an increase in drug use, but in a social group other than that thought to be most 'at risk', then the preparations may be quite inappropriate.

2. *From disbelief to shock*   When drug use (and in particular, heroin use) *does* manifest itself within social networks – neighbourhoods, friendship groups, families – then one initial response of those non-users who care about the welfare of the new users is almost always one of shock. In

the central section of this chapter, we describe the ways in which this shock manifests itself for many parents, and then go on to discuss the various ways in which 'the problem' becomes defined and worked through within the context of the immediate family and friends. The focus here is upon the mother's reactions and the ways in which she construes this problem in the context of child socialisation. The issues thrown into sharp relief by heroin and other drugs will be familiar to many mothers – coping with uncertainty, anger, guilt and exhaustion – but there seems to be something specific about drug problems that sharpens these feelings.

3. *Resources available shape longer-term responses* In the longer term, parents and other family members may try out a variety of ways of responding to a drug user in the family – or in some cases may stick with their first response. The strategies eventually settled upon depend not only on the parents' sense of right and wrong,[3] but also on the practical, personal and community resources that they have at their disposal.

One of the most important resources that parents have at their disposal in the longer term is the network of neighbourhood and community contacts and relationships to which they have access (cf. Bulmer, 1986). Another resource is access to a range of services – statutory services (health, police, etc.), non-statutory services and, in the case of the better-off, private health and welfare facilities (such as private drug rehabilitation houses). The closing sections of this chapter describe how these resources (external to the family) are brought into play in a variety of ways depending upon the opportunities provided by a particular neighbourhood, its history (general and drug-specific) and the ability of social groups to draw upon these.

We begin, then, with a descriptive account of a community in which heroin is expected to surface at any time, but as yet, has apparently failed to do so.

A town lies in wait

Yuppiesdale is a small industrial town in rural East Anglia. It is a town preparing itself for a problem yet to manifest itself, for whereas at least one neighbouring town is known to have an escalating heroin problem, so far Yuppiesdale has apparently been passed by. Nevertheless certain sections of the community are already gearing themselves up for what they fear is the inevitable and probably imminent arrival of a heroin problem in the area.

The history of the town gives us little clue to explaining why it might be a 'late developer' in relation to heroin problems. During the 1960s its population increased threefold when the Council, concerned about the exodus of its young people, began to implement a Town Expansion Scheme in conjunction with the Greater London Council (GLC) rehousing people from London's East End. Today there is still a strong London connection, with those who are unable to find local employment commuting to the city. A legacy of this development is that, unlike many rural areas, Yuppiesdale now has a disproportionate number of people under 25 years old. Perhaps because of the way that it has developed, Yuppiesdale tends to be seen as the trouble-spot of the county and a town which perhaps has more in common with some urban areas than the rest of the surrounding area with its 'county' outlook. It may be this, coupled with its youthful population and London links that, in the eyes of observers, appears to make Yuppiesdale a likely candidate for a drug problem.

Despite its history, or perhaps because of it – it is essentially a town without noticeable extremes of rich and poor, very much a place of the 'middling' classes, aspiring working class and undistinguished lower-middle classes – the townspeople describe a strong sense of community and strong family and friendship networks through which local news travels. It is this that leads people to assert with some confidence that if Yuppiesdale already had a serious drug problem then they would know about it. Local parents seem concerned, but hardly agitated about drugs in general or heroin in particular, although there is concern about under-age drinking in the town. There are no local branches of national organisations concerned with drug abuse – the nearest branch of Families Anonymous (some thirty miles away) folded when the professionals worker who was running it moved away.

Evidence from official sources supports the popular view that the town does not have a serious drug problem – at least as far as heroin is concerned. In the past year, local police reported only two cases of arrest where drugs were involved – cannabis in both cases. Similarly, health workers report no evidence of heroin use, although there is some suggestion that amphetamine use (including injection) may be on the increase. There is only one notified heroin addict in the town, who is well known to all statutory sources and regarded as something of a curiosity. The town's only real experience of dealing with a drug problem was two years ago when glue-sniffing and solvent abuse became a visible problem and was accompanied by an increase in shoplifting. In this instance the town rallied to confront the problem. Members of the public were active in informing the police of glue-sniffing activity and local shopkeepers, encouraged by concerned professionals, responded by restricting the sale of glue and some other sniffable products.

In this situation, where there is little direct experience of heroin and most people's knowledge about the drug is obtained at second hand, the media play a strong role in shaping local perceptions. While the national press and the government anti-heroin campaign have undoubtedly played a part in putting drugs on the agenda, the local press went one step further, declaring the town to be a site for major dealing in drugs: 'Drug Shock – Opium sold in town for £17 000'. This report concerned the supposed sale of $4\frac{1}{2}$ ounces of opium on the streets of the town. The information, which was credited to the Drug Squad, was later denied and a disclaimer issued but by then the story was already the talk of the town. Indeed much of the rumour circulating around the town seemed to originate in remarks made by police officers. This seems also to have been the pattern in other areas before officers become familiar with drugs as a matter of routine police work, lacking in glamour; they subsequently mature into more diffident witnesses.

Reflecting the popular perception of drug problems being varieties of *youth* problems, the practical preparations for the anticipated arrival of heroin were largely initiated by the town's Youth Service. In 1985 Yuppiesdale's Youth Worker called a meeting on drugs, inviting representatives from local professional and community organisations with an interest in young people. At this meeting, an inter-agency group was formed, and began to meet regularly. Initially, members of the group saw their role as preparing and educating themselves for a problem that had not actually arrived. However, their contact with the Drug Squad suggested that the problem was already in Yuppiesdale. 'They told us that the real hard stuff is in Yuppiesdale now' reported a member of the group. This report, together with the national publicity about heroin and young people, encouraged the inter-agency group to set up a drop-in service to provide Samaritan-style advice and counselling to young drug users and their families. The main instigators of the service were the Youth Worker and a senior Clinical Medical Officer responsible for schools in the area. The Youth Worker, although unable to provide any concrete evidence for his concern, was aware that there was a lot of talk among young people about drugs and where you could get them. He saw the drop-in service as a preventive measure – if people were talking about it, then the next step might be doing it, and it was best to be prepared.

The proposal for a drop-in service was by no means universally supported. Both the education authority and the local police attempted to block the idea because they were anxious that issues might be raised at a time when their own organisations were not geared up to respond. However, prestigious medical backing provided legitimation to what would otherwise have been a low status proposal (the Youth Service is not an object of awe for many other agencies). The Clinical Medical Officer, who had previously worked in an area with a high level of heroin use agreed to provide clinical back-up to the service. The interest of the Clinical Medical Officer was reinforced by developments within the health service at local and national levels. Regional and District Health Authority members reflected popular concern and anxieties generated by the media. These anxieties were articulated as 'there must be a problem, what are you going to do about it?' The Health Authority was also under some pressure (as were all other Authorities) from the DHSS, which had issued a Circular suggesting that services should be appropriate to local need but (at that time) gave little indication as to how the need might be assessed. Officers of the Authority were therefore somewhat in the dark about how to proceed when instructed to prepare a report on the drug scene in the district. The report, which was compiled in great haste (three weeks) suggested that although there was a drug problem it was perhaps not as great as some had feared. The report estimated that there could be 120–175 heroin users in the District Health Authority, 15–20 of these being in Yuppiesdale. The figures for Yuppiesdale were generated purely on the basis of population figures and information from other areas, rather than from any direct evidence from the town itself. Other aspects of the 'evidence' presented in the report were based on speculation and hearsay. For example, a teacher estimated that 25 per cent of secondary-school pupils had used cannabis, and this seems to have been accepted in the report without any substantive evidence. Nevertheless, the report sufficed to reinforce perceptions of the need for a youth-orientated drug service in the town.

The drop-in advice and counselling centre was opened on youth club premises for a trial period of ten weeks from February 1986, staffed by a part-time youth worker. By the end of its trial period, the drop-in service had had eight callers, the majority of whom had not come out of concern about a drug problem. Even those who had presented themselves as drug users were more concerned with personal, family or employment problems. This disappointing (or reassuring) response dampened plans to set up a permanent provision of this kind, the instigators concluding that the town did not need this type of service at that particular moment. Evidently, whoever might have been using drugs in Yuppiesdale either did not have any problems relating to their use, or else did not find this particular service attractive.[4]

In spite of the limited catch of the drop-in centre, the town continued to be rife with speculation and rumour about places where drugs and drug users might be found. We interviewed a variety of professionals, voluntary workers and 'ordinary' lay people (adult and adolescent) and found that three elements recurred in the folk-knowledge of where the problem might be located: (i) the places where young people congregate, particularly the local motor-bike-shop-turned-cafe; (ii) public houses, numerous sources suggesting cannabis at least is freely available from a number of pubs in the town; (iii) the 'worst estate in town' – the assumption being that if there were a drugs scene anywhere then it would probably be there, because of the estate's general reputation.

In our interviews and group discussions, we found a good deal of misinformation about different types of drugs and the signs of drug use in all sections of the community, including amongst professionals. The topic of drugs and young people seemed to us to function as a bit of mildly arousing, commonsensical, disapproving, conversational tittle-tattle: 'Yes, well, they would, wouldn't they, young people today, and if they haven't yet, well I dare say that they will do soon, and then things will be very bad indeed!'

This representation of a problem – as something which is potentially devastating to young people and yet not dangerous at present because it is far away – describes the mood of parents and others in the community, not only in Yuppiesdale but also in other areas in Britain where the problem has yet to manifest itself. In the following section of this chapter, we describe how this brittle sense of security – safety in distance – can shatter. Friends, relatives, parents and especially mothers of those young people who are discovered to be using heroin, may be quite appalled.

Case study: a problem in the family

How can and do parents, in particular, respond when what seems to be a distant danger is found flourishing at home?

Parental responsibility and family self-help loom increasingly large in the rhetoric of social policy in the 1980s. Responding to drug problems is one area in which these ideas are deployed. But little is really known about what these ideas might mean in practice – other than that it is women who are the focus of both the ideology and practice of family self-help.[5] In the following paragraphs we explore some of these issues, showing how parents generally, and mothers specifically, respond to a drug problem in the family in a variety of ways. Sometimes these responses involve adopting ready-made discourses on 'parents and drugs', and sometimes they involve drawing upon personal, cultural and neighbourhood resources to painstakingly construct their perspective on the problem. Many parents feel strongly that they have no relevant personal experience on which to draw when it comes to drugs. There may be a desire for someone to tell parents how and what to think about drugs, and how to find a way of placing these unfamiliar issues within a familiar framework. For many parents, therefore, the *first move* is not necessarily towards other parents, but towards state agencies and professionals who can, it is hoped, deal with the problem on their behalf.

If one wishes to expand the theme of parenting, then one can think of these as people who, sensing that they cannot cope, search out a secular father- or mother-figure to succour them. More broadly, this pattern can be seen as one of 'clientisation' – both for the parents and for the child – and as a taking-up of state promises of welfare and law and order (Jagger, in preparation). Many parents who take this route, however, find themselves disappointed by what the state seems capable of delivering in practice, as the following case study, drawn from our research in 1985, shows.

Pauline and Colin

'Pauline' first became aware of her son's involvement with illegal drugs some three years before she found out he had progressed to heroin. Initially, on discovering Colin was using cannabis. Pauline's reaction was to ring the local Drug Squad, in an attempt to get them to take action against the pub which was well known locally as the source of supply of a wide range of drugs. When the Drug Squad failed to act she rang Scotland Yard. At this stage she also involved relatives, who had the reputation of being 'tough nuts' and were regarded with some esteem by her son. The relatives were invited to a family meeting and as Pauline put it, gave her son 'a good talking to'.

Later, as it became more and more apparent that Colin had a serious drug problem, Pauline sought 'softer' forms of outside help, initially contacting the Samaritans, but eventually finding her way to a parents' support group run by a local drug agency. Relieved of some of her initial fear and isolation, Pauline – thinking of a way of giving her son a new sense of pride and purpose – bought him a car. Shortly after, Colin wrecked the car. Pauline again turned to outside help and through her GP arranged to take her son to the Drug Dependency Unit (DDU).

The visit to the DDU resulted in Pauline adopting a strategy which up to this point she would have found unthinkable. DDU staff told her that, in order to be accepted as a patient of the clinic, Colin would need to have heroin in his body. This being the case, Pauline was told she had two choices. Either she could leave it to her son to obtain his heroin – stealing in order to obtain the necessary money – or Pauline could help him to obtain his regular supply. Fearing for her son's safety, Pauline not only provided the money to support his habit but also drove him to and from deals during the period he was awaiting acceptance by the clinic.

In the event, attendance at the clinic proved not to be the answer Pauline had hoped for; Colin continued to use heroin while receiving methadone on prescription. Feeling this was the last straw Pauline told him to leave the family home. He has never returned and although Pauline knows of his whereabouts she has had no further contact with him.

The desire to impose control on the child by involving outside help from statutory agencies very often comes up against an apparent impossibility of eliminating drug use by direct surveillance, at least without some cooperation from the user him/herself. If the family cannot rely on such cooperation, there may be intense frustration with the user, which relates also to the different perspectives of the people involved:

> they don't see what they're doing. We see, but they don't, so you have a particularly difficult situation.

Even when cooperation and communication occurs for a while, experiences of relapse and recurrent feelings of being let down by the user may lead parents to feel intense despair and hopelessness. In reaction, they may at times feel like rejecting the user.

As might be expected, the mother is likely to be the prime mover in developing strategies for responding to a drug-using son or daughter. Husbands and other children sometimes pull in the same direction as the mother, sometimes in different directions, and sometimes try to withdraw altogether. Mothers often describe fathers as unable to cope, or as having a limited repertoire of responses and this can put a strain on the relationship between the parents. This may be especially difficult if mothers see their responsibility for child-care as of primary importance. Those siblings who try to support the mother or both parents can get deeply involved in a variety of ways, some of which are regarded as helpful by one or both parents, and some not. The resulting conflicts and confusions can add considerably to the initial problem.

*   *   *

There are a number of ways in which one could describe the various ways in which parents develop their strategies; for ease of illustration, we have chosen to divide the remainder of this chapter into three main parts. In the first of these, we describe the general perspective and some of the strategies recommended by Families Anonymous, which has become an important source of knowledge, advice and personal support to those parents who identify themselves primarily *as parents* when constructing their responses to their drug-using sons and daughters.[6] Subsequent sections will describe some patterns of response which are premised upon parents positioning themselves as members of a local *community in struggle*, engaging in collective action to clear the problem out of their immediate environment; and as *clients of the state*, trying to give the problem to state agencies such as the police or the health service.

These accounts raise a number of social policy questions. For example, in responding to the issue within the family, are parents shouldering their responsibilities in the way that central government policies would advocate? In doing so, are they acting as an alternative or substitute for state action? Or do they see themselves as acting out of a sense of disillusionment with the services available from the state, whether doctors, police, or teachers? Are the models of family support and action which parents are developing ones that parents are inventing for themselves, or do they simply accord with central government views of family life? Is it parent power in alliance with the state, or in defiance of the state, or a series of accommodations and negotiations?

Parents drawing upon the resources of the 'parents movement'

Drug use, particularly drug use by young people, upsets a lot of people. It particularly upsets parents of the young people concerned. Starting, then, with those adults who position themselves primarily within a discourse on parental identity, responsibility and rights, we can ask – what does parenthood mean?

There is a growing but quite diverse literature on social reproduction and cultural reproduction, child socialisation and mothering,[7] and some of this has been useful to us in thinking about the blow that drugs seems to inflict upon the practice of parenthood. Drawing upon this literature, we can say that, as parents in this culture, we expect to pass on a family name as well as various elements of our physical, social and personal characteristics. We may also self-consciously build up cultural and economic capital to pass on to our children – and we expect them to receive it happily and gratefully in whatever form it may be offered. For parents, then, there is an expectation of a line of continuity between themselves and their children. This quite basic, often implicit, expectation may be contradicted by a number of experiences among which, for whatever reasons, drug use (particularly heroin use) looms large.[8]

How do these issues relate to parents' reactions to illegal drug use by their children? Drug use by young people is felt by many parents to represent a severe form of discontinuity in the life of the child as they thought he/she would become, at times amounting to the death of the child. There are also real fears for children's physical safety. Parents may see the child as being locked in a process of self-destruction, or this perception may alternate with the feeling that it is the parent herself who is somehow destroying the child:

> What I felt was, what can be the matter with me, what am I doing destroying my own children, the last thing I want to do and it's happening (mother).

Thus parents may feel that they have failed the child – 'where did I go wrong?' – at the same time as feeling that the child has betrayed the parent – 'why has he or she done this to me?'

For mothers, there is in addition the special significance of the mother–child relationship, which for some at least constitutes a core part of identity. Boulton (1983) has shown how women may enjoy motherhood for its immediate satisfactions, but may also gain an important long-term sense of meaningfulness, believing that whether or not their mothering seems to be valued in the present, it will be in the long term because of what or who the child will become when he/she grows into adulthood. Frustrations in the immediate experience of motherhood are made more tolerable because they can be set against a long-term perspective of the fruitfulness of mothering.

More generally, Hilary Graham has discussed the significance for women of acts of caring, a caring which Graham describes as a labour of love. In this, she is seeking to convey an understanding that the labour and the love which constitute caring are inextricably interlinked (Graham, 1983). Both sides of the equation – the labour that has gone into producing the son or the daughter, and the caring feelings that legitimise such work – are made a mockery of when parents come to regard the child as being a 'drug user'. The initial shock and sense of stigma may be followed by a period of grief and mourning at the loss of the child as they had envisaged he/she would become, together with fears for the imminent loss of the child in a tangible physical sense and recriminations against themselves and/or the child. When these initial reactions begin to be replaced by exploration of ways in which the parents might try to regain contact with the child and to find new ways of caring, there may be bewilderment as to how this should be expressed. What is the labour that is appropriate to this form of breakdown in family life?

One answer to these dilemmas is given by the loose association of parents' groups subscribing more or less directly to the ideology of Families Anonymous. In this case, the key idea is that care needs to be redirected from too tight a focus upon the child, to a revaluation of the parents themselves. This is an assemblage of ideas that can all too easily be interpreted as saying that there is nothing that parents can do to stop their children's drug use. It is in fact more complex than this, containing a number of elements that are not entirely mutually consistent, as we shall show. Some of the key ideas are as follows.[9]

Self-control   In this approach the emphasis is upon controlling yourself rather than the user (or anyone else for that matter). It is rooted in a philosophy that suggests that we can only take charge of our own lives, and that this is where our responsibility lies. In addition, drugs problems are seen as constituting a 'family illness' that requires all members of the family to recognise the extent to which they collude in, and thus perpetuate, the pattern of misuse. Parents are advised to change their own behaviour and create space in which the user will have the opportunity to change him or herself. The correct parental response is one that is directed towards the parents' own recovery. If there are beneficial consequences for the user, then this is of course to be welcomed, but it is not the main aim of the strategy.

Tough love As a term, 'tough love' is widely used and indeed a number of different people claim to have originated it. In some respects it may perhaps be seen as contrasting with 'permissiveness':

> If you're a soft touch you just add to the problem. You've got to bring discipline into your own life as a parent, and you've got to learn to love them.

Love and understanding do not entail acquiescence to whatever a child wants:

> I'm going to stand here like a rock and not budge, and you can come back to me when you feel like it . . . That's real understanding . . . To say 'I really understand you, I don't mind what you do', that's not real understanding.

So part of the self-control entails the aim of ceasing to 'enable' the user. To this end parents refuse to collaborate in any actions that might make it easier for the young person to avoid the consequences of his/her drug use.[10] Could this in a sense be a more subtle and indirect form of power – the power of inaction or withdrawal of labour?

Powerlessness Nevertheless, the third major strand of FA philosophy concerns the theme of powerlessness. Parents are asked to affirm not only that they are powerless over the lives of others but, also, that they are powerless over their own lives and should therefore seek the help of a higher power – however that is conceptualised. Nevertheless, as the theme of self-control suggests, this is not meant to lead to an abdication of responsibility by parents. Indeed, the major part of the programme of FA is concerned with parents' and others' responsibility to reassess and reconsider their own actions. But this responsibility can only be exercised by seeking the aid of a higher power:

> You are powerless over drugs and other people's lives, which is a tremendous relief . . . It was out of my power. I was completely helpless, there was nothing I could do.

Such sentiments appear to have little in common with themes of parental authority and assertion, and may look ill-at-ease next to an approach of tough love. However, what this perhaps highlights is the indirect nature of the powerfulness of tough love. Powerlessness over others is expressed in a refusal to enable, and is thus transformed into the powerfulness of the refusal to act and to collaborate.

The practical responses developed by parents under the influence of FA may not always accord completely with their 'theoretical' rationales. For example, FA (and indeed many other groups and individuals) advocate a model of drug-use-as-an-illness, and the appropriate response to illness would normally be active caring. Yet FA also advocate a strategy of non-directiveness and self-control – not something which would normally be seen as an appropriate response to illness. Consider the following extract from a mother – not a member of FA but a subscriber to the general view that drug use is a kind of illness – which illustrates this:

> There we were with sick children, but whereas when they were kids and they had measles or a cold or ear infection, you knew exactly what to do to help them through their illness, here we were faced with a sick child and [were] totally incapable of bringing them any help at all, other than by doing the naughty things we occasionally did – like buying them a bottle of codeine, or giving them an extra fiver, knowing damn well that extra fiver was to go on a fix.

In describing the ideology of any movement, including that still strengthening parents movement around drug problems, one should allow for some flexibility, hence apparent mismatch, between what is done and representations of it. It could even be argued that a totally consistent model might in fact not be the strongest one for coping with the contradictions and complexities that confront a family in crisis. This is partly because adoption of a strategy for responding to one's son's or daughter's drug use is not a once-and-for-all event, but an extended period of *angst* and struggle. Mothers and other relatives may find that their moods and responses chop and change abruptly at times; they may alternate and shift between different strategies, or use a combination of several.

Unless family members have some wider resources upon which to call – an ideology that revalues them themselves, a supportive set of relationships in the immediate community or neighbourhood, or access to services that make sense to them – they generally find it very difficult to surmount their difficulties. Having looked briefly at the first of these resources, as articulated by the British parents' movement around drugs, let us now look at one example of the second.

Public activism as a context for parental care

One of the resources available to parents is the example of what other parents can be seen doing in the public arena. In communities where the identification of a serious drug problem has promoted a variety of vigorous responses, family members' development of a strategy may be heavily influenced by what other local families seem to be doing – by what is popular.

'Tenantsrise'

This case study concerns a locality (or rather, a socially linked set of localities) in a large town in north-west England. Here local conditions have favoured a very rapid build-up of drug problems and an equally rapid and very public collective response. Let us begin by sketching in the background, and then describe how family members utilised existing forms of social organisation to mount their 'counter-attack'.

The Tenantsrise estates are located within a borough of mixed housing that has returned both Labour and Conservative councillors in the past. The working-class end of the borough in which the Tenantsrise estates are located strikes a contrast with the more affluent part, and this physical differentiation is matched in the minds of Tenantsrise residents by a sense of social identity emphasising the strong communal and collective aspects of working-class culture. The main focus of collective activity is the network of tenants associations in the area, around and out of which have arisen a number of community projects and groups, including networks that underpin the struggle against drugs. A majority of the activists are women, and this aspect marks a continuity with action within the family. But the form of their action – a good-humoured but combative series of autonomous actions and demands upon state agencies – provides quite a contrast with the depressive and privatised modes of coping that characterise parents responses to youthful drug use in some other areas of the country.

The built environment in Tenantsrise not only stimulated the main form of social organisation, tenants associations and their spin-offs, but also helps to explain the public nature of the heroin scene locally, and hence the public response. The estates generally conform to a pattern – rows of houses and maisonettes around parts of the perimeters, with a number of medium-rise and several high-rise blocks in the middle. The stairwells of the medium and high-rise blocks provide opportunities for groups to congregate out of the public gaze.

From 1985 heroin dealers and users became noticeable in first one and subsequently other parts of Tenantsrise; throughout that year the problem escalated in a very obvious way. Crowds of young people would congregate around the estates at set times, pick up one-dose 'bags' of heroin from small dealers ('with the stuff in shopping baskets!' as one tenant described) and then disperse to use the drug. Many of them, wishing to use the drug before their return home, entered the stairwells of the blocks and stayed for about half an hour, usually in groups of five to ten. This caused considerable upset and annoyance to residents – and to caretakers, who had to clear up afterwards. A group of caretakers – talking about the scene on one of the estates, from which heroin had largely moved on by 1986 – gave us this picture:

Well I happened to be working on the back stairs the next day and I noticed the stuff on the back stairs like.

Interviewer: What was that?

You get sick as well, vomit, cans of coke lying around, bars of chocolate, things like that. They don't eat the chocolate, they use the silver paper, and they throw the chocolate away and use the paper ['chasing the dragon', a method of smoking heroin].

Everybody knows the signs.

Oh, aye, yes.

Interviewer: Where do they get that knowledge from?

Well, I mean – they . . . its obvious.

Interviewer: Its not obvious to everybody, you know.

Well no – it is in these flats, because if you see a group of fellows that don't live here and they are about 18 or 19 and are walking around in the lifts and are on the landings, its obvious what they are up to . . . we [caretakers] come up and down and say 'what are you doing here?' and they say 'oh we were waiting for someone', that's the first thing they say to you. And you say, 'who?'. And they can't answer you, who the name is. 'Oh I'm waiting for Billy So-and-so'. And you say, 'well, he doesn't live on that floor'. And its bloody obvious . . . we have known right away.

Yes . . . you smell them . . . Its like a firework that has been let off . . . Silver paper and matchsticks, bars of chocolate, bottles of water . . . candle grease . . . saves using matches.

As seen by Tenantsrise residents, problems could be identified along several dimensions:

(a) The mess: no one liked the mixture of matches, foil, body fluids and so on that was left at the scene of intoxication.
(b) Fears: many residents, particularly pensioners, felt intimidated by the sheer presence of so many young people.
(c) Violence: in some cases, residents who protested directly to prospective users or to dealers were threatened in no

uncertain terms. This shut some people up, but it made others angry enough to want to do something.

(d) Police inaction: police seemed reluctant to act on information received.

This matrix of problems, facing a group of people who had already developed a form of social organisation – tenants associations – drew a very rapid collective and public response. Meetings were called, local leaders emerged and were supported, a series of demands were made upon police, health and welfare agencies and the Council building department, and these demands were articulated publicly through local newspapers. Direct action also took place, involving confrontation between young people 'hanging around' and groups of residents. Some residents also engaged in quasi-vigilante activity such as congregating outside the houses of 'known dealers' to harangue them. Many of the residents involved simultaneously struggled with the problems posed for them by their own son or daughter using heroin. As recounted to us, although this was a very resting period it had its positive side in drawing people together and stimulating a strong community feeling between families in their neighbourhoods.

At the time of writing (summer, 1986) clear achievements could be identified by Tenantsrise residents. The publicity generated may *initially* have made the problem worse, by drawing in more petty dealers and prospective users from other areas; but the residents' shouting, haranguing and determined surveillance of 'their' estate, plus some police activity that they elicited, did help to 'move the problem on'. Their biggest success was undoubtedly to get the Council to knock down and rebuild parts of the estates that gave the greatest opportunities for drug use, and to carry out simple measures, such as the fitting of entry phones to other blocks. These were the sorts of improvements for which the tenants associations had been pressing for years, but it took the public scandal of drug use and the additional energies that this mobilised for them to be able to press the argument to a successful conclusion.

As rebuilding occurred and many tenants were relocated to other parts of the city, some initiated anti-drug action in their new communities, virtually none of which were free of heroin. These people formed a cadre of community activities and moral entrepreneurs, and currently constitute a force to be reckoned with. Their actions have not defeated the heroin problem in the city, indeed one might observe that availability and use has now become more generally dispersed over a broader area; the local police believe that this may be one of the consequences of vigorous action against low-level dealers. Nor have all the children of activists totally disengaged with heroin – some have, some have not, some are 'inside' (in prison) so no judgment can yet be made, and a small number have died. In the following case study we illustrate how this situation was expressed by one of the mothers whose children became involved with drugs.

A mother and an activist

For 'Maggie' and her family, the pattern of discovery and response embraced a more diverse and upsetting range of crises and confrontations than many parents have to face. Their experiences have had an influence on the ways in which other local families have coped with a drug-using teenager, yet ironically it was because of the earlier growth of a spirit of neighbourhood vigilance that the son of the family first 'got into trouble'. Local drug dealing had reached a scale where old people were scared to go out and parents were extremely worried about their young children getting involved. Calls for police action followed. Having had no idea of her son's activities, it was a great shock to Maggie when the police arrived on her doorstep saying that they had arrested her son Michael and his girlfriend for possession of as yet unidentified drugs. They had been called in by a neighbour who did not realise the young man was Maggie's son.

When the drug was analysed it was found to be a mixture of heroin, talcum power and gravy powder. Being told that this was an extremely dangerous mixture, perhaps potentially lethal,[11] upset and angered Maggie. As the incident was already public and in the hands of the police she thought that Michael's stupidity deserved to be punished: 'I said, you can keep him; anyway he went to court and got fined. I made him pay it for himself because he was working.' After what the family hoped would be a lesson to Michael, Maggie asked him why he had become involved with heroin. She and her husband had provided a good home and what Michael was doing made 'no sense'. Michael explained it as 'going along with the boys' and got very upset.

As in other families, Maggie's responses developed from the initially guilty reaction of asking 'where did we go wrong?', to trying to keep an eye on Michael and get him to drop the 'bad company' with whom he was associating – in particular his girlfriend Sue. But Maggie's strategy for dealing with her son's heroin problem also took seriously the question of where he was getting the drug itself. She took the issue outside her own home and family, discussing it with neighbours, raising the issue with the Council and vocally demanding that action be taken against 'the pushers'. Her public remonstrations did not stop Michael or his friends using drugs, but it did have an impact on them – making them think about what they were doing.

Maggie's next move was to try to develop better cooperation and coordination between parents in the same situation as herself. While continuing to keep an eye on Michael within the family, and encouraging a 'stable' life-style by ensuring that he kept going to work, Maggie teamed up with other mothers with drug-using sons and formed a Family Support Group. The group grew quite quickly and helped to mobilise tenants' action against local dealers, as well as agitation about broader environmental problems such as housing decay and poor sanitation. The group also helped Maggie's family and others to translate the initial reaction of trying to cope with a drugs problem solely within the family, into a cooperative effort which embraced a form of treatment for the young users which all the parents approved. An acupuncture clinic, based in the centre of town, had offered its services to the parents. Maggie's group organised themselves to overcome the major difficulty that might prevent the young people from going to the clinic, distance, and borrowed a mini-bus to take the kids to the clinic, working a rota to sit with them during their treatment and to make sure that they got back home all right without straying.

Unfortunately, despite all this activity at the level of both the family and the community, Maggie's own story did not quickly move towards a happy ending, since Michael was arrested for a minor (non-drug) offence and sent to prison. She believes that the strategy that she and other local parents worked out does seem to be having some effect on local users and dealers and her optimism for the future is based on this and on the feeling she gets from Michael's letters from prison that 'things will be different now'.

This sketch of an 'activist' points up the importance of having support from a wider network of friends and neighbours close at hand – a network which can not only give aid in relation to care and control of the child, but also funnel some of the parents' anxieties, energies and hopes outward into broader, often more manageable and rewarding activities.

What the stories of Maggie and of other Tenantsrise parents represent, then, is not a victory over the heroin trade, but a public and full-hearted engagement with its local manifestations. Local community organisations have been able to force certain accommodations both upon state agencies (housing, police) and upon drug dealers and users. Their public action, drawing upon existing collectivist traditions and organisational forms, contrasts quite sharply with responses in other areas, which were often state-led, privatised, and low key. It is to two such cases that we now turn, before rounding off the chapter with a description of the intermediate possibility of state–parents cooperation (and the contradictions and conflicts that this can provoke).

State and professional initiatives

In these paragraphs we describe two settings in which state and professional initiatives in relation to drug problems, rather than parental or other lay activism, is the dominant feature. In the *Marginsville* case study, state agencies and their professional staff seem to have retained 'possession' of the issue, largely because of lack of parental or other lay organisations that might have laid claims. In the second case, *Helpsborough*, by contrast, the agendas of parents and professionals have begun to diverge. In neither case are the parents the prime movers (as in *Tenantsrise* or – to give a different example – in parts of the USA, Linblad, 1983).

Marginsville

Marginsville is an overspill area on the edge of a town on the south coast of England. Here, state services for drug users are relatively well developed, and community responses undeveloped. This balance of responses reflects a relatively long history of health services responses to drug problems in the general area, and a lack of community organisation onto which a 'popular' response to drug problems could be grafted.

Demographically, the area of coast in which Marginsville nestles is marked by a relatively large retired population, attracted by the facilities of the area, reasonable climate and reputation as a respectable location for respectable folk. Interspersed with the retired are other populations connected to the industrial base of the area (holding up relatively well), the service sector (enlarged by leisure and communications), professionals and a student population. The result is a relatively heterogeneous set of social groups, but little general sense of 'community' as an actively integrating and energising process. Hence there is little of an established framework of community linkages in which a lay public response to drug problems might readily lodge.

As far as the state's response to drug problems is concerned, things are relatively well developed. The geographical situation of the surrounding area and the good links with continental ports may have contributed to the development of a small-scale drug importation and dealing scene (locally, and as a part of the London-focused trade) from the 1960s onwards. A Drug Dependency Clinic was established in 1968 and since that time a framework of services, involving both statutory and non-statutory sectors, has evolved. The general impression obtained from people whom we interviewed in the statutory and non-statutory sectors was that a coordinated response was in place and functioning tolerably well. However, this response was a bureaucratised rather than popular one, and the involvement of ordinary members of the community was relatively low, being restricted to the attendance of a small number of parents at support groups organised by professionals in a neighbouring town.

Interviews carried out with tenants, caretakers and shopkeepers in Marginsville confirm this picture. Whilst there is drug use, including heroin use in the locality – a fact confirmed by a GP, drug advice workers, probation officers with clients resident in the area, police, probation and some residents – most of this use is relatively discrete and privatised, taking place not in large publicly visible groups but in the homes of individuals. In some cases, individuals resident on the estate go into the centre of the town to obtain drugs, certain pubs being known as places of supply. A pub on the outskirts of the research area had become quite widely known as a place for dealing in stolen goods and illegal drugs (other than heroin), and this notoriety led to it being closed. But generally speaking drug users do not usually congregate publicly in large groups or in ways that might identify them as users (in distinct contrast to users in Tenantsrise).[12] Perhaps there is a feature of the drug distribution system in this region of the country that reduces dealing of drugs to younger adolescents, and hence reduces the likelihood of public displays that might stimulate a higher level of community response. But, as we have indicated, the relatively heterogeneous population and lack of extensive social ties outside the family may also contribute, as may the relatively highly developed system of statutory and non-statutory specialist services. These features of the area, its history and present development combine to create a situation in which it is the state, rather than any 'community', that leads local policy on drug problems.

Helpsborough

Our final case study is set in a borough on the western outskirts of London, where the presence of a statutory agency has provided the focus for a community response by parents and relatives of drug users. Previously we noted that Marginsville's response to local drug problems is dominated by the statutory and non-statutory services and that of Tenantsrise has been by lay community action. In Helpsborough however we find a more mixed situation, where lay and professional interests are still being played out and have yet to be reconciled. But before we look at the nature of this uneasy alliance we take a brief look at the setting.

The borough has a long history of heroin use. It is claimed that the seeds of the problems were sown by a local GP who started treating drug users, privately prescribing opioids. Some say that his action helped to make an existing, although relatively small problem, much worse. Others argue that he merely served to highlight the real situation – one where heroin use was already extensive but not recognised by service providers. The failure of the statutory services to respond to the problem is still reflected today in the lack of local provision for drug users. At present those wanting treatment face long delays for appointments and a 15-mile trek to the nearest Drug Dependency Unit.

Nevertheless in 1984 the availability of government funding, together with the borough's reputation as a problem area in relation to drugs, led to the setting-up of a specialist drug agency under the auspices of the Youth and Community Service. Reflecting its position within the Education Service, the role given to the new agency was one of education and prevention; its staff, who were all from a youth-work background, have no brief to work with the large number of adult drug users still to be found in the borough. In practice the workers found this situation fraught with conflict, finding it impossible to ignore the needs of drug users, especially when the possibilities for referral elsewhere were limited. Within a short time workers found themselves with two jobs – their official job and another that was being carried out in their own time. It was in the context of this unsatisfactory state of affairs that the idea for a separate, independent organisation arose, and in Spring 1986 a local branch of Aid for Addicts and Families (ADFAM) was formed. The new organisation was mainly based on an existing relatives' support group run by the statutory drug agency. Although it was clearly professionals who provided the initial impetus, the relatives were quick to take up the idea. Many had had personal experience of the difficulties involved in trying to get help for a drug-using member of their own family and, having gained confidence from the support group, were willing to try to do something to improve the situation.

In retrospect it is clear that both between professional and lay members and among lay members themselves there was little consensus about what the new group should be doing. The professional workers (the staff of the drug agency) saw the group as a source of personal support and as a pool of volunteers to offer help with befriending, transport, fund-raising and other activities which they were unable to carry out, either because of their position as council employees or simply through lack of time. The workers' expectations of the group therefore might be most accurately described as something akin to a 'league of friends', a situation in which lay members support the work of the professional staff, the direction of activities being determined by the latter.

The lay members, however, had other ideas. Perhaps because of their social class background (the group was largely drawn from the working-class end of the borough), lay members did not easily align themselves with middle-class notions of volunteering. Many felt that the new organisation should take on an active campaigning role. In particular they felt that efforts should be directed towards establishing a new Day Centre which would offer help to those wanting to come off drugs and continuing support to those who had already undergone treatment. Like the professional workers, they believed that while there were still so many long-term users around who needed to deal in order to support their habit, it was inevitable that young people would be drawn into drug misuse, despite an active prevention programme. Also, some parents, weary of the task of dealing with their (ex-) drug-using relative, saw the prospect of a Day Centre as a source of help *for themselves* and a more concrete solution to their problems than the once-a-week relatives' support group offered by the statutory agency.

However, even amongst the lay members, there were disagreements. Some felt that the task of setting up services for users was too big to take on and that *relatives*, rather than users, should be the focus of attention. In this case the objective was seen in terms of setting up a telephone line offering twenty-four hour advice and support to parents and other relatives. At the time of writing, the group was still divided and some members, frustrated by the lack of progress were talking about forming a breakaway group.

For the professional staff, the nature of their relationship with the lay community has been thrown into question by these unexpected developments. Despite its own internal disarray, the 'support group' has distanced itself from its instigators and gone its own way – almost like some wilful adolescent. Far from being a source of unproblematic support, the group now threatens to pursue objectives which, in the eyes of professionals, are at best unnecessary and at worst positively harmful. A Day Centre, which enables addicts and ex-addicts to socialise is not, they argue, the solution to the problem but the way to create a new one.

Conclusion

The relationship between families and the state has been a crucial issue in social policy since the nineteenth century, and the question of drug abuse by young people has edged this relationship further into the spotlight. We are not in a position to develop any general theory of the relationship between family members and the state. Theories extant include that of Donzelot (women family members in alliance with state agencies, to the detriment of the family); those of the radical-feminists such as Firestone (male oppression of women being conducted through both state and family) and, rather differently, Delphy (married women having class interests opposed to those of husbands because their household work is given free); of socialist-feminists (women's work in the home cheapening the cost to capital and/or the state of reproduction of the labour force); and of Parsons (the family functioning to reproduce the social structure).[13] Although these accounts cannot be reconciled into one perspective, each contains provocative insights that articulate the concerns and experiences of certain social groups. There is, therefore, no general theory of state and family that can be regarded as generally accepted at the present time. Indeed, we doubt that any discourse on state and family could ever amount to a *general* theory, however compelling it might appear at certain times (Foucault, 1980).

Social policy issues arising from parental and community responses to drug problems must be seen in terms of a meeting of discourses, none of which is hegemonic. From the perspective of the state, as articulated by the present administration, the issue is one of 'parental responsibility'. This perspective has informed the recent development of policy in the fields of crime control, education, social welfare and health care generally. Parental responsibility in relation to youthful drug use is seen as a specific instance of the more general theme – supporting a particular version of the family, reducing demands on state services, and reducing inefficiencies and immoralities at community level by encouragement of forms of self-reliance that stay within the law.

At the same time, however, the Conservative administration came to power on a political programme that gained part of its popularity by pointing up a breakdown in law and order and by drawing attention to threats to the person and property posed by delinquents and criminals. This tendency to 'stir the pot' of public anxieties in relation to criminality and disorder finds a reflection in government announcements on the drug problem, with repeated assurances that we are in imminent danger of being swamped by cocaine imports (heroin being by now more familiar, if not exactly cosy, in the eyes of the British public), drug suppliers and traffickers being described as serious criminals akin to terrorists, and drug users being portrayed (for example in the England and Wales 1985/6 and 1986/7 anti-heroin campaigns) as helpless victims, reduced to moronic social garbage. One can ask whether this recent tendency to 'talk up' the seriousness of the problem is compatible with the longer-term policy commitment to encourage people to feel that they can cope and can 'take responsibility' for the problem. Although discourses on parental responsibility are very much to the fore, their own manifest contradictions restrict their power to capture and assimilate the thinking of all social groups – each of which brings forward its own concerns. It seems reasonable, therefore, to expect there to be a variety of popular 'readings' of the government's intentions and also a variety of responses.

This is what we found in our research. From the perspective of lay people – parents and other relatives of users, friends and neighbours, their contacts in the lay community and with helping agencies – the government's intention is only one of the factors to be taken into consideration when trying to work out how to respond to drugs at a local level. As indicated in preceding sections of this chapter, parents and others have a variety of resources available to them, depending upon their economic and social position, demographic and cultural features of their locality, family structure and dynamics, personal experience and so on.

What does this imply, as far as the practitioner, citizen or policy-maker is concerned? Simply that any individual, group or agency wishing to understand or to make an intervention into drug-related problems at local level needs to be alert to a range of related issues – personal resources (including gender and motherhood) of individuals; family structure and resources (including access to services); features of the local community (especially the extent to which there are active non-drugs networks onto which drug-related activities can be mapped); history and current organisation of state services at the local level, and inputs from the national context; and the ways in which these are worked through. If this seems to make things more complicated than expected for the practitioner, planner or policy analyst who seeks a clear statement about the national patterns of parental and community response to drug problems, then we can only reply that their expectations were unrealistic. Family and community responses to heroin and other drugs are like most things in life – complicated.

Notes

1. 'Parental and community responses project' carried out by ISDD with funding from a charitable trust. The project resulted in a book for parents, reflecting their concerns in their own words: *Coping with a Nightmare*. For publication details please contact the Publications Unit, ISDD, 1–4 Hatton Place, London EC1N 8ND.
2. 'Identifying neighbourhood heroin problems', a project carried out for the Department of Health and Social Security. We gratefully acknowledge the support of the Department for this project. Please contact ISDD for publication details of report, *The Limits of Informal Surveillance*.
3. It may seem unprofessional of us to use such terms as 'right' and 'wrong', but such terms do reflect something of importance to our respondents, and something that is not adequately captured by lukewarm concepts such as values or beliefs.
4. In the event, our own research indicated that heroin was indeed to be found in Yuppiesdale. Independent lay sources told us that people on several of the estates had some experience of use of the drug, and that one medium-sized dealer was well established in the summer of 1986. The lowest estimation of numbers of users was around ten, and one respondent suggested that around fifty users were being directly or indirectly supplied by the one dealer and as many people again having some experience of use of the drug. The types of persons said to be involved were primarily young middle-class adults – 'yuppies'. However, all our attempts to meet directly with these hidden users were rebuffed, our go-betweens indicating that their contacts saw no advantage and quite some risk in such contact with outsiders. We cannot therefore be sure of our facts in this case. But it is a salutary thought that whilst the focus of

professional concern and development of services was orientated to potential teenage users, a quite different social group has been at play.

5. Self-help in relation to sexual divisions has been discussed by several authors. See, for example, Finch and Groves (eds) 1983.

6. There are a number of other groups besides Families Anonymous (FA) active in relation to drugs, including OPUS (Organisation of Parents Under Stress) and ADFAM (Aid for Addicts and Families). The focus here on FA is in no way intended as depricatory of these other groups.

7. Some examples are: Aberle and Naegele (1968); Backett (1982); Badinter (1981); Boulton (1983); Bourdieu and Passeron (1977); Delphy and Leonard (1986); Graham (1983 and 1984); Kohn (1971).

8. Exactly *why* drug use and particularly heroin use functions as such an effective 'interruptor' in family life is a complex question not addressed in this chapter. We do not feel that it is sufficient to make reference to 'moral panics' or to any other explanation which assumes that individuals and social groups assimilate any way of thinking and feeling offered to them through the media and other channels. The question must be posed – why is it that certain panics and pleasures are so popular with certain constituencies? Obviously, the contemporary practice of parenthood has its vulnerabilities (a series of accidents waiting to happen, some might say) but why is it that these are no neatly targeted by drugs/heroin? To say that the reason is simply that drugs are so horrendous circumvents the question.

9. This description of the strategies of Families Anonymous represents our own interpretation, and is based on written material produced by FA, such as 'The Twelve Steps', and also on interviews with members of FA groups, obtained as part of the Parental and Community Responses project.

10. See Bill, 1980.

11. In fact, such mixtures of powers are likely to cause considerable problems if injected, but if heated on foil then of course, only the volatile constituents would be ingested.

12. We found one exception to this general rule, as described by a caretaker of a block of flats in Marginsville. Referring to a single woman and two males living in a flat, the caretaker gave his opinion that 'she was definitely pushing. A stream of different kids going up there to the flat. You wouldn't get that many kids going to one flat for nothing.'

13. See Donzelot (1980); Firestone (1979); Delphy (1977); Seccombe (1974); Parsons (1954).

5

From treatment to rehabilitation – aspects of the evolution of British policy on the care of drug-takers

Susanne MacGregor and Betsy Ettorre

Drug use is a common social activity, the motivations, methods and consequences of which are shaped by a variety of historical, cultural and political forces. Similarly, official responses to drug taking are influenced by those same forces, whether or not they are socially visible. It is beyond the scope of this chapter to analyse in detail how these social forces have operated over time or their level of impact on the development of treatment and rehabilitation policies. We simply describe current treatment and rehabilitation policies and ask if they represent a rational response appropriate to the realities of the 1980s and to the new wave of concern with heroin misuse in Britain.

Drug policies in the 1980s: achieving priority status

Concern about drug misuse has grown steadily in the 1980s. In the space of one or two years, policies regarding drug misuse have been elevated to priority status and the drug issue is recognised as a major social problem. In June 1984, the DHSS circulated forceful 'guidance' to health authorities declaring that 'Ministers now regard the improvement of services for drug misusers as of the highest priority', of equal importance with service development for the elderly, the mentally handicapped and mentally ill. The Government now considers that 'the development of services for drug misusers must remain a high priority for the foreseeable future' (DHSS, 1985).

An investigation by the Home Affairs Select Committee (1986) in 1985–6 led to its first report *Misuse of Hard Drugs*. This Committee visited Amsterdam and The Hague; New York; Washington, DC, and Miami – as well as the Channel Islands. Perhaps as a result of what they heard on these travels, the Home Affairs Committee phrased its report in relatively alarming language: 'Drug dealers . . . threaten us all, including our children, with a nightmare of drug addiction which has become a reality for America' (Home Affairs Select Committee, 1986, p. vi). They declared that 'immediate and effective action has to be taken if Britain is not to risk inheriting the American drug problem in less than five years' and 'everything possible [should] be done to try to avoid what has occurred in the USA' (Home Affairs Select Committee, 1986, p. viii). Earlier the Chairman, Sir Edward Gardner, had referred to the drugs problem as an epidemic, a plague, the 'most serious peace-time threat to national well-being'. Reference to the 'Americanisation' of the problem refers not only to its size but to an intractability where drug taking becomes a way of life for the under-class in 'no-go' ghettoes, where crime, from the Mafia to street thefts, permeates everyday life and public affairs to an extent not yet known in Britain. Some observers fear they see this on the horizon. Statements such as 'I have seen the future and it is frightening' are reflections not just on drug misuse in British society, but on our social structure and on everyday life in decaying urban areas.

How serious is the drugs problem in Britain?

The crisis of drug misuse has two dimensions. There *is* a crisis, we would argue, if crisis is defined as a condition which cannot be remedied without fundamental structural change. This crisis is the result of the coincidence of two features:

1. the nature and size of the problem – that is, the increase in drug taking and the increase in the problems associated with drug misuse;
2. the failure of the existing treatment system and the inadequacy of the current response.

The rate of increase *is* serious and a cause for concern, if not quite the 'grave illness and terrifying social evil' described by Bernard Braine in the *Daily Telegraph* (14 April 1984). A review of the character of the situation in the 1980s compared with previous decades highlights:

- the centrality of illicitly imported heroin;
- the importance of organised criminal operations in the importation and distribution of the drug;
- more widespread knowledge of and contact with drug taking, no longer confined to marginalised, outcast groups;
- high growth-rates outside London (starting from a lower point and escalating noticeably, thereby causing particular difficulties where it occurs in areas with an absence of services);
- and some concentration of the problem among younger working-class youth on estates or in deprived inner-city areas (see Chapter 3, this volume).

The increase in supply reflects a vast increase in world-wide production which shows little sign of abating (see Chapter 2, this volume).

Increased availability and use obviously increases the numbers likely to experience problems. Even if the present 'epidemic' were to wane 'naturally' as the 'vulnerable group' became saturated or as a clamp-down on supply proved effective, we can expect increases in the number of 'problem drug takers' for a number of years ahead. An upsurge produces a ratchet effect so that demand for treatment and care does not fall back to the previous lower level. This group will continue to make demands on services for some considerable time.

An indication of the national pattern is provided by a recent study by Glanz and Taylor (1986) on the increasingly important role of GPs in the treatment of opiate misuse. This is evidenced by rising proportions of all first-time notifications resulting from the statutory duty of medical practitioners to notify the Home Office of addicts who come to their notice. These rose from 29 per cent of all notifications in 1975, to 49 per cent in 1980 and to 55 per cent in 1984. From this survey of 845 GPs carried out between May and August 1985, an estimate of 44 000 *new* cases of opiate drug misusers consulting GPs in 1985–86 has been produced.

This is the tip of the iceberg. What proportion of all opiate drug misusers consult a GP in any one year? Is it likely to be all of them, a half or a quarter? One in five GPs comes into contact with an opiate-drug misuser during any one month. This indicates the important role already being played by GPs and their crucial position in any future development of services. In *Guidelines of Good Clinical Practice* (Medical Working Group on Drug Dependence, 1984), the circular distributed to all GPs by the government, the principle was stressed that 'it is the responsibility of all doctors to provide care for both general health needs of drug misusers and drug-related problems, as they would for patients with other relapsing conditions'. Additionally, the idea that drug users are a heterogeneous group was stressed as a principle of treatment. Linked with this principle is what emerges from many studies: the crucial distinction between drug taking and drug misuse, that is, a difference between *experimenting* with drugs (occasional, intermittent, recreational drug taking) and *getting into trouble*, developing problems, becoming dependent or addicted (through regular use of heroin for example). In discussing explanations for these patterns and in formulating policies, it is of the utmost importance to keep clear this distinction. There is no one solution, and policies for the one are inappropriate for the other.

Treating heroin addicts: the development of the 'British system'

Much of what we discuss in this chapter regarding changes in services providing some form of care for drug users acknowledges the influence of what has been called the 'British system' of prescribing heroin to 'addicts'. The term 'British system' is, perhaps, rather misleading, since it suggests that consistent planning has accompanied the development of policies and practice and has led some commentators to oversimplify and eulogise the British approach (Trebach, 1982). Compared with the history of drug policies in the United States, in which enforcement has played the primary role in attempts to contain heroin use, the British approach appears relatively liberal and medicalised. But it should be remembered that it is only in respect of dependent users of heroin (and other opiates, and to a lesser extent, cocaine) that maintenance-prescribing has been a feature of the British response. Against occasional (non-dependent) users of opiates and against users of other drugs, the British system has resorted to law enforcement just as the United States has.

The British system of maintenance prescribing is, then, *part* of the British control system rather than its core. As the Advisory Council on Misuse of Drugs observed:

The controls over drugs of addiction introduced in the United Kingdom in 1920 preserved the right of doctors to prescribe for the purpose of medical treatment, thereby enabling them, if they thought it right, to prescribe controlled drugs to addicts. This principle was, however, soon questioned and subjected to detailed review by a Departmental Committee (the Rolleston Committee) [which] laid down guidelines as to when it would be appropriate to prescribe morphine or heroin to addicts:

a. when undergoing treatment for the cure of addiction by the gradual withdrawal method;

b. when, after every effort had been made to overcome addiction, the drug could not be withdrawn completely, either because withdrawal produced symptoms which could not be treated satisfactorily under the ordinary conditions of private practice (i.e. other than in a hospital); or because the patient, while capable of leading a useful and fairly normal life so long as he took a certain non-progressive quantity, usually small, of the drug of addiction, ceased to do so when the regular allowance is withdrawn.

These guidelines, which were accepted by the government of the day and the medical profession, thus provided the foundation of what has since become known internationally as the 'British System', i.e. the management of an addict by the prescription of maintenance doses, often over a fairly lengthy period (ACMD, 1982, pp. 7–8).

Subsequently, the right to prescribe opiates (though not the right to care for drug users in other ways) was restricted to doctors working in a setting in which a comprehensive range of services appropriate for addicts could be provided. Modification of the British system resulted in the establishment of NHS Drug Dependency Units – 'drug clinics', as they are more popularly known.

The restriction of prescribing to the clinics can be traced to several concerns around changing patterns of availability and use of opiates in the mid-1960s. These included changes in the user population with the emergence of younger, working-class male users (Jamieson *et al.*, 1984, p. 4) alongside older users – generally those who had become dependent in the course of medical treatment with opiates or who had had some kind of professional access to such drugs and developed a problem after recreational or experimental use. The new, younger users were seen as a disturbing challenge – not adults and not 'respectable'. It was in response to their emergence that the 1965 report of the reconvened Brain Committee called for the provision of 'suitable' units for the treatment of drug addiction, stating that:

> each centre should have facilities for medical treatment, including laboratory investigation and provision for research. A centre might form part of a psychiatric hospital or of the psychiatric wing of a general hospital (Interdepartmental Committee, 1965, paragraph 22).

The provision of such facilities, combined with stricter controls over the supply and availability of opiate drugs, was intended to contain the spread of addiction. The clinics were to be under the direction of consultant psychiatrists, backed up by nursing staff. The new system gave each consultant control over her or his clinic's policy, and allowed the clinic psychiatrists as a group to maintain a united front against the involvement of ordinary GPs in the treatment of dependent persons. For a while, the clinics generally adopted a fairly liberal prescribing policy, attracting a large proportion of existing users – who had hitherto obtained their heroin from doctors no longer authorised to prescribe it. However, during the 1970s the clinics moved away from prescribing injectable heroin or methadone, substituting the relatively unexciting orally taken methadone, almost invariably on a schedule of reducing dosage. Partly for this reason, a smaller proportion of heroin users today obtain their supplies in a legitimate way, from doctors, than was the case twenty years ago.

The clinics remain an important feature of the statutory health and welfare response in Britain, having been supplemented by a variety of non-statutory services such as rehabilitation houses and street agencies. The following paragraphs describe the emergence of these services.

The emergence of rehabilitation as an adjunct to treatment

Reassessment, debate and deliberation have consistently surrounded the development of treatment and rehabilitation policies for drug misusers. Prior to the 1980s, policies in this area implied a dichotomy between treatment and rehabilitation, as noted by the Advisory Council on the Misuse of Drugs (ACMD, 1982). For example, treatment was restricted to the medical setting of the clinic, while rehabilitation (a non-statutory agency response) was regarded as a more active process, encouraging self-determination and personal integration as well as the development of social skills and interpersonal relationships. In practice this dichotomy created an unnecessary gap within the treatment and rehabilitation system.[1] As a result, two parallel approaches emerged: on the one hand, an individualised containment-cum-confrontational approach adopted by statutory agencies such as clinics; on the other a self-help community approach supported by non-statutory agencies (Jamieson, Glanz and MacGregor, 1984, p. 12).

The roots of this dichotomous way of thinking can be found in the Second Brain report (Interdepartmental Committee, 1965), two 1967 Ministry of Health Memoranda (Ministry of Health 1967a, 1967b) and the early work of the Advisory Committee on Drug Dependence (ACDD, 1968). The Second Brain report (Interdepartmental Committee, 1965) called for the establishment of special centres with facilities for medical treatment of drug addicts. This report also noted that details for the organisation of and provision for facilities for 'long-term rehabilitation' were 'outside their terms of reference'. Although a concern for rehabilitation was seen as necessary if relapse was to be prevented, the primary focus of concern was on treatment arrangements: the drug clinics. The subsequent publication in 1967 of two Ministry of Health memoranda, *The Treatment and Supervision of Heroin Addiction* (Ministry of Health, 1967a) and *The Rehabilitation and After Care of Heroin Addiction* (Ministry of Health, 1967b) outlined action taken or proposed on the recommendations of the Second Brain report. The former memorandum described treatment facilities which hospital authorities were asked to provide for persons addicted to heroin, while the latter provided the already promised guidance on joint planning by regional and local health authorities for establishing rehabilitation and after-care facilities for discharged patients. While close collaboration between hospital authorities, local health authorities, general practitioners and non-statutory agencies was emphasised in the second memorandum, *both* memoranda implied a distinction in principle, if not practice, between treatment and rehabilitation.

It was during this particular period in the formation of British drug policy that an official document mentioned non-statutory (voluntary) bodies in this field for the first time. This very casual mention occurs in the introduction to the second memorandum:

> The form of possible arrangements has been discussed by the Department with psychiatrists experienced in the treatment of addiction, and with Medical Officers of Health and voluntary bodies having a special interest in this subject (Ministry of Health, 1967b).

At that time, rehabilitation was seen to involve two elements: the re-education of the individual to living without drugs and the development of social resources, including trade training and settlement in employment (social rehabilitation). It was believed that while the combined responses of treatment and rehabilitation would be complementary, only a small proportion of addicts would want long-term rehabilitation. Thus, treatment arrangements appeared again as the primary focus of concern.

The slow rise of rehabilitation

A more detailed view of rehabilitation, involving a variety of disciplines and services, was presented in the ACDD report on *The Rehabilitation of Drug Addicts* (1968). It was within this report, put forward by the ACDD's Rehabilitation Subcommittee, that rehabilitation, conceived as beginning with an addict's first contact with an out-patient clinic, was recognised as a *special need* rather than a *mere adjunct* to treatment as implied in previous documents. With the brief 'to consider the various ways in which rehabilitation of persons dependent on drugs can most effectively be arranged by statutory and non-statutory agencies' (ACDD, 1968, p. 1), the Subcommittee's key recommendations included: the establishment of hostels providing short-term accommodation for homeless addicts attending out-patient clinics; input from social workers at various service levels (in-patient, out-patient, and after-care); planning for special hostels developed on experimental lines; the encouragement of voluntary bodies to pool their experiences and to discuss their plans and the need for local health authorities not only to set up hostels themselves or assist those run by voluntary agencies but also to provide support (both financial and advisory) in these developments. 'Good communication' on all levels was stressed and special mention was made of the positive contribution of the courts, prison service and probation in rehabilitation. The contributions of these agencies were subsequently addressed in more detail in the *Report on Drug Dependents within the Prison System in England and Wales* (ACMD, 1979), a report submitted by the Working Group on Treatment and Rehabilitation and endorsed by the full Council, then the ACMD, in 1979.

The concluding statement of the *Rehabilitation of Drug Addicts* report suggests the need for cooperation between treatment and rehabilitation services:

> there should be a multi-disciplinary approach to the problems of prevention, treatment and control . . . there should be close cooperation between treatment and rehabilitation on the one hand and the police and courts on the other, and continuous care for the patient should be maintained by the same therapeutic team throughout (ACDD, 1968, p. 23).

This sentiment was resurrected in part by the ACMD (1982) when the need for a comprehensive approach, with treatment and rehabilitation linked as key elements within a long-term multi-disciplinary response, was stressed. On the other hand, the ACMD's 1982 report appears to reflect a shift in the official way of thinking. Indeed, by recognising the 'traditional' dichotomy between treatment and rehabilitation as 'counter-productive' and 'unrealistic', the ACMD appears to part company with its predecessors. For example, the need, put forward in 1982, for 'active involvement of a wider range of specialist and non-specialist agencies' (ACMD, 1982, p. 43) and the requirement for 'a programme of integrated treatments and a variety of agencies working with the client or patient over a period of several years' (ACMD, 1982, p. 35) challenges the 1968 view that 'addicts are to be cared for consistently by the same therapeutic team' (ACDD, 1968, p. 23). The subtle shift here is the movement towards a more comprehensive treatment and rehabilitation policy which attempts to ensure conditions for cooperation between statutory and non-statutory agencies. Both sectors of care are to be seen in equal partnership, supporting drug misusers.

Perhaps the shift towards a comprehensive response should be expected, given the pressures which service providers had experienced because of the changes in the nature and extent of the drug problem in Britain during the 1970s. Nevertheless an indication of a shift towards this way of thinking was recorded as early as 1967 when the view that 'getting the addict back into work and a settled way of life is an immensely more difficult problem than drug withdrawal' (Anonymous, 1967) was put forward in the *British Medical Journal*. Similar views (Expert Committee on Mental Health, 1967; Office of Health Economics, 1967) held at that time suggested the need for a full response involving a wide range of agencies.

Given all this, what was actually happening? What sorts of practices, policies and assumptions were being challenged by drug users and drug workers within both the statutory and non-statutory sectors of care?

The focus moves from heroin to multi-drug use, and back to heroin

While a major focus of policy concerned with drug addiction has been the Drug Dependence Unit (Smart, 1985), doubts about the efficiency and appropriateness of the clinic system arose within two or three years of its inception. Fuelled by pressure from the non-statutory sector and from a few key consultants and social workers, concern was expressed about the prescribing function of clinics, about drug misusers who were not being seen at the clinics (because they were not dependent on opiates) and about pressures on Accident and Emergency departments and street agencies (Ghodse, 1977, 1979 and *et al.*, 1981).

In both the clinics and the non-statutory street agencies, the rather gruesome fixing-rooms set up soon after the inception of the British system became displaced. While the strict enforcement of rules linked with the formalisation of treatment plans played a key part in this displacement, reduction in the amount prescribed and the switch from injectable to oral methadone were also crucial factors. Significantly, the notion of long-term maintenance was abandoned and it was assumed that patients would be willing to work towards abstinence. New programmes introduced in the field were based on psychological theories of social learning. Stimson and Oppenheimer (1982) see these changes in the 1970s as a response to the frustration felt primarily by staff at the clinics. Regardless of the reasons for these practical changes in and around the clinic system, key assumptions were challenged throughout the 1970s. Professional and lay opinion increasingly questioned:

- the definition of 'the addict' in terms of the substance taken, rather than as someone for whom drug-taking overlaid and exacerbated other 'problems in living' and who might be better viewed as a 'multiple drug misuser' or 'problem drug taker';
- the dominance of the clinics and psychiatry in determining models of practice while techniques of therapy and rehabilitation, such as counselling and therapeutic communities, were playing an increasing role within both the statutory and non-statutory sector;

- the appropriateness of prescribing a dangerous drug especially on a long-term maintenance basis while the objective of health-care workers was a drug-free, healthy life;
- the limitations of a purely 'physical' conception of problems while drug misusers faced considerable difficulties with housing, employment, child-care and treatment in prison;
- the assumption that services are best organised on the basis of a sharp distinction between the stereotype of the 'junkie' or 'addict' and other more 'normal' patterns of drug use (for example, of alcohol, tranquillisers, etc.).

It is ironic that just as these challenges had been absorbed into the orthodoxy of the policy and practice of key decision-makers and had been set out in the ACMD report on *Treatment and Rehabilitation* (1982) a new wave of heroin addiction swept over the country and reinstated older notions of epidemic and danger, centred on one substance – heroin. While informed experts and practitioners in the small, closed circle of the 'drugs field' had come to agree on notions of 'problem drug taking' and the need for a 'multi-disciplinary approach', this professional consensus was swept aside as politicians and the public demanded that doctors should 'do something' about this pernicious evil.

The clinic system under strain

The clinic system was under considerable strain well before the current concern and attention was devoted to the drugs problem. Problems soon arose with this 'system' – which only in its earliest years looked much like its image, especially that held abroad of it as a maintenance-based, medical rather than social or criminalising system. For a start, only certain types of patients received treatment. Especially as doctors switched to oral methadone treatment programmes, large numbers of drug takers remained outside the clinics. What was happening to those who did not attend, or who attended for a short time but did not stay? Some were not treated at all. Some received treatment from GPs or from private doctors, evidenced in the vast increase in the number of notifications from GPs relative to clinics and prisons. Others found their way into the non-statutory sector. The non-statutory (or voluntary) sector developed rapidly to fill the gaps in the tight, restrictive state sector. In spite of the recognition of these problems by workers in the field, the authorities still felt able in 1978 to claim with some satisfaction that 'in comparison with several other countries facing similar problems, the UK appears at present to have a relatively stable situation as far as narcotic drug dependence is concerned' (Central Office of Information, 1978).

Yet by 1980 a *Times* leader could comment, 'the present machinery of drug-addiction clinics, registration of addicts, maintenance dosage and drug replacement is not for some reason competing adequately in the eyes of many customers with the market' and urged a re-examination of 'the effectiveness of our containment policy towards hard drugs' (13 August 1980).

A joint letter to *The Times* (23 January 1981) from a conference of representatives of the clinics and the non-statutory sector referred to the marked increase in the number of people seeking help for problems caused by drugs in the previous two years and pointed out that GPs were once again undertaking the care of opiate addicts. The letter noted the long wait involved in gaining admission to detoxification units and argued that the trend toward devolving the funding of services to local level must be reversed. Central government should accept the financial responsibility for provision of the core costs of specialist drugs services. As the letter argued:

The effect of local funding where competition with more attractive client groups is unavoidably direct is to exclude many drug addicts from specialist care. . . . Increasingly local funding has come to mean the withdrawal of support from resources and personnel.

The long list of forty-five recommendations in the ACMD report on *Treatment and Rehabilitation* (1982) form the basis of the current consensus on responses to the problem. They include reference to the principle that provision should not be substance-centred nor even diagnosis-centred but should focus on problems, and that policy responses should utilise not only the full range of specialist services but also other statutory services – social work, youth services, housing and employment; that regional and district multi-disciplinary drug teams or advisory committees should be set up; and that there should be more and improved training. The ACMD further commented: 'if there is to be an adequate response to the undoubted increase in problem drug taking then additional funding must be made available both at local level and from central government'.

The ACMD Report on *Prevention* followed two years later. It listed thirty-two recommendations which included a suggestion for limits on prescribing and a call for health education at a broad level. More training was called for. It concluded that the Home Secretary should assume specific responsibility for the coordination of policy on prevention of drug misuse at national level and reaffirmed the need for drug advisory committees at local level, which should include representatives from education and the community in addition to psychiatrists, community psychiatric nurses, and social workers. Since then the Social Services Committee has queried whether these committees, which do seem to have been established in most areas, might not degenerate into mere 'talking-shops' (Social Services Committee, 1985).

Current government strategy and the Central Funding Initiative (CFI)

Tackling Drug Misuse (Home Office, 1986) presents current government policy on drug misuse. First published in March 1985 and updated in March 1986 to take account of a whole range of further initiatives, this strategy document aims to attack the drug problem of five fronts, one of which is 'improving treatment and rehabilitation'. While the thinking of the ACMD informs much but not all of this presentation, part of Section 7, 'Treatment and Rehabilitation' (specifically paragraphs 7.4 and 7.10) indicates a shift towards non-medical community services which has widened the range of possibilities under discussion in the 1980s (see, for example, Strang, 1985).[2]

The Central Funding Initiative (CFI), a key element in the government's current strategy, may be seen as a way of remedying some old problems and rising to new challenges. Nevertheless, while the CFI was, in Norman Fowler's words, 'the government's initial response to the ACMD Report on Treatment and

Rehabilitation' (DHSS, 1982) it has supported the increase in community-based services *without* establishing clear lines of vertical coordination from national to local level. The problem of lessening the gap between national and local levels and establishing the need for an alternative approach was voiced subsequently by the minority statement contained in the ACMD Report on Prevention (ACMD, 1984, pp. 79–83).

The total sum now expended through the CFI is estimated at £17.4m (Coomber, 1986). The Social Services Committee commented, however, that 'while good enough as far as it goes [the CFI] is totally inadequate as a governmental response to a rapidly growing problem' (Social Services Committee, 1985, para. 99). They recommended that the DHSS 'create a central fund for services for drug misusers to which Regions could apply; that it should use the accountability review process to chase up those Regions which do not show interest; and that it should exercise close control over the way in which these funds are spent' (Social Services Committee, 1985, para. 101). The Government's response to this, however, was to point to the pump-priming boost of the CFI and to reiterate that 'it is not the function of central government to determine local needs and make decisions about local priorities and the best way of meeting local needs. Health and local authorities are in the best position to make these judgements' (DHSS *et al.*, 1985).

It is still early days to see the impact of the CFI on the shape of services nationally or to evaluate whether or not this 'key element' has offered a viable solution to a growing problem. Regardless of the further injection of £5m per year from 1986 available to health authorities and additional to the CFI (DHSS, 1986), we are left with the fear echoed by the Standing Conference on Drug Abuse in their memorandum submitted to the Social Services Committee, that:

> in three years' time, at worst there will be a significant reduction in services. At best, there will be such financial uncertainty that some voluntary organisations may not be able to continue and others will only survive at considerable cost to the staff, the service and most particularly, to people with drug problems (Standing Conference on Drug Abuse, 1985, para. 6.9).

Criticism of existing services

The Social Services Committee in its Fourth Report commented on the 'woefully inadequate' state of existing services for the treatment and rehabilitation of drug misusers. The final paragraph of this report encapsulates much of the informed current concern about services for drug misusers:

> The misuse of drugs, and particularly misuse of heroin . . . is a serious and growing problem. It demands an immediate, determined response from government . . . Existing services are woefully inadequate to cope with the increasing pressure. Treatment facilities are few, underfunded, often inaccessible and always with long waiting-lists. Rehabilitation is provided, if at all, by voluntary organisations unable to plan ahead for lack of secure funding. Experienced staff are in very short supply . . . Recent initiatives, national and local, are welcome but not enough . . . Most local and health authorities are apparently unwilling to give any degree of priority to services for drug misusers. The Government must put forward a clear long term strategy for the coordinated development and maintenance of services for drug misusers . . . New money will be needed . . . Training facilities for specialist staff of all disciplines must be increased greatly . . . Drug misuse can be tackled but only if expressions of concern are matched by action (Social Services Committee, 1985, para. 105).

To these statements could be added the following specific comments:

- opening hours at clinics and other services are often inflexible and do not suit everyone;
- homeless people find particular difficulty in receiving primary health care;
- the concentration on heroin in general policy discussion and in the response of the clinics gives insufficient attention to other substances, especially tranquillisers;
- those with children need special attention and facilities geared to their needs;
- there are major shortages at key points in the treatment

process causing problems of access and blockages, especially
in relation to detoxification facilities;
- too often services seem to be provided on the basis of the
  preferences and inclinations of particular units or staff, thus
  providing some limited variety in services but a variety which
  is not necessarily best suited to the needs of all those in the
  catchment areas;
- there is evidence of stigmatisation of patients and clients;
  once they are defined as drug takers, they may be denied
  access to general services.

This indicates one of the costs of setting up special services for
problem drug takers, insofar as practitioners in the general
services (in health, education, social work) tend to feel absolved
from responsibility or they feel that the problem is necessarily
too complicated for them to be able to deal with. The
compartmentalisation of services leads to a lack of continuity and
comprehensiveness of care and many fall through the gaps.

A pragmatic approach: a full response linked with the awareness of gender and race

If we start from where we are now, deal with the problem as we
find it, with the resources we have available – that is adopt a
pragmatic approach – we find that the available expertise is
concentrated in the clinics and in the non-statutory or so-called
voluntary sector. Throughout the 1970s there was and in some
areas, remains, an antagonism between these two. But staff in a
number of areas have broken down the barriers and developed
coordinated action, as in the north-west, Tyneside, and
Bloomsbury, based upon a philosophy shared among consultants,
social workers, nurses and community workers.

This is one model for the development of services. It sees clinic
staff as playing a key role, coordinating, training, acting as a
catalyst but aiming to utilise a wider range of services – from GPs
and community psychiatric nurses to health visitors and probation
officers. Of course, an equal partnership with the non-statutory
sector would be aimed at. Day centres and rehabilitation houses
would all be linked in to provide a comprehensive network of

services for drug misusers, which could see the client through from first contact to final 'settlement' in a home and a job on completion of rehabilitation. Such a vision of a network of services in each area would include a 24-hour, 7-day a week crisis intervention and detoxification unit, and advice and counselling, out-reach work, day centres, clinics and a variety of rehabilitation houses or residential accommodation with different regimes for different needs or inclinations.

Any new model should include a concern for the needs of special groups such as women and members of the black community who are under-represented quite strikingly in the current service provision for drug misusers. The 1985 DAWN survey (DAWN, 1985) of 254 London agencies highlighted the inadequacy of the current response with regard to the issues of gender and race. Briefly the six main findings were:

1. only 100 of the 254 projects surveyed made any particular effort to help women with drug/alcohol problems;
2. although all the 100 agencies surveyed were thought to be aware of the specific needs of women clients, eighty-three agencies responded that women clients had needs or problems different from men. Of the eighty-three agencies responding that women had special needs, eighteen agencies were unable to state any actual needs or problems specific to women;
3. only about one in four agencies recognised women's particular problems with child-care and housing, while less than one in five accepted that women face discrimination in treatment. (This latter finding did not square with the experiences of women themselves, reporting at DAWN open meetings);
4. only fifty-one agencies were able to specify what, if any, further facilities they felt were needed for women. Although the ACMD had expressed concern about the long-term prescription of minor tranquillisers to women, only one agency in the whole of the metropolis showed an awareness of the need for greater provision in this area;
5. despite the fact that London is a multi-racial city, many agencies responded as if cultures other than white European ones did not exist. Only one in twenty agencies saw more than 10 per cent black women or women of colour. None of the specialised drug/alcohol coordinating agencies offered any

analysis of racism and of the problems faced by people from different cultures;

6. statutory facilities (Drug Dependence Units and Alcoholism Treatment Units) showed the least understanding of women's needs and were the most difficult group from whom to obtain responses.

Although DAWN made recommendations on the basis of these findings, there is still a lack of response in the addiction field to the needs of women with children; women users of tranquillisers; women of different cultures who experience problems with alcohol and/or drugs; and women problem drug takers and drinkers in prison or on parole.

The question of the effects of institutionalised racism or sexism on the overall provision of services is an important area of concern. A pragmatic approach would begin to reform existing services to make them more flexible in response to special need groups, as well as maintaining and developing forms of provision designed expressly and exclusively for specific groups (such as women-only services). Sensitivity to social groups, cultures and special needs could be a starting-point in providing better services for *all* drug takers. The exact shape and form of services – who would take the leading role and so on – however, can only develop organically over time in each locality, depending on the people active in that area and the level of local awareness.

Conclusion

In its Fourth Report, the Social Services Committee concluded that the situation is 'genuinely alarming', that 'overcoming drug dependency demands more of a social than a clinical approach' and that 'an immediate, sizeable and recurring injection of additional money by the Department (DHSS) is essential' (Social Services Committee, 1985, vii, ix, para. 100).

The crisis facing us at present provides an opportunity to develop a fresh approach to tackling the drug problem, an opportunity for debate to develop among the various authorities about their contribution. When the dust has settled, what will turn out to have been the outcome of this critical phase? A truly innovative new approach? Or just patching and mending? Or worse, neglect?

Should Local Authorities play a role? The Social Services Committee commented: 'few local authorities have much of a clue as to how to deal with this social problem, which has come to be seen as either medical or criminal and few feel obliged to take any initiative'. Yet it is clear that, because of the increase in the number of problem drug takers, the specialist services cannot cope alone. The clinics are overloaded and experience staff shortages. They are unable to meet the demand for immediate care, let alone take a central role in the development of services and involve themselves in training and education. GPs and probation officers are under pressure and need training and support. Their key problem is lack of confidence and lack of knowledge. Drug taking has to be demystified so that primary care workers and generic service workers feel willing and able to accept responsibility and to take on the care of drug takers, rather than being content to refer them to other services. However, they need also to be able to recognise when the situation is more complicated and it *is* appropriate to refer on to more specialised services. Here, too, more training and support services are required. Local Authority Social Services Departments are already involved in casework with clients with drug-related problems, and can work more closely with the voluntary agencies, GPs, clinics and probation officers to develop a coordinated response. Models such as those developed in Southwark and Islington may be illuminating (see, for example, Working Party on Drug Abuse in Southwark, 1985).

One danger facing local initiatives is that drug misuse could become a political football between central government and local authorities and an opportunity to develop a fresh approach could be lost. The key issue is that of the financing of services for drug misusers. But together with this, it is still essential to consider the best use of money available (given that resource constraints are likely to be with us for some time) and the best use of the talents and skills available. From 1987 onwards, the three-year projects funded by the CFI come to the end of their term. Will these services attract sufficient local funding to survive – or will they go under because Local Authorities and Local Health Authorities will not or cannot pick up the bill? Will the late 1980s see an injection of central government funding into both Health and Local Authorities? Or will government choose to continue to directly fund (and hence more directly shape) at least some drug services?

The wider issue has to do with offering alternatives to drug taking and escapism for the beleaguered generation of the 1980s. Through the education service, training and employment, sport and leisure, cultural activities, and the youth services, efforts have to be directed to rebuilding broken communities. But the areas with the worst problems are those with the least revenue. Hard-pressed local authorities and Health Authorities find it difficult to put services for drug misusers ahead of those for, say, kidney transplants or old people. While youth have been damaged directly by the current recession, other groups, such as women and black people have also borne the brunt of the cut-backs. It is time we paid more attention to the needs of each of these neglected groups.

Notes

1. For a fuller discussion of the effects of this dichotomy on the development of non-statutory agencies see Ettorre (1987).
2. British services are predominantly centred on a 'reformist' model of drug use and appropriate responses. The reformist model uses a rehabilitative approach, stipulating a change of life-style. The ultimate aim is a drug-free existence. The 'addict' is seen as an individual with a behavioural problem. For a discussion of three dominant philosophies (medical-model, reformist or libertarian) see Rosenbaum (1985). For a discussion of the centrality of the reformist model in Britain see MacGregor (1986).

6

Reconciling policy and practice
Nicholas Dorn and Nigel South

In this final chapter we draw upon those preceding and examine the prospects for the development of policy and practice in response to heroin problems. As the preceding chapters have shown, Britain's heroin problem in the 1980s has grown out of changes in structural circumstances (factors in international trade, developments in the domestic economy in Western countries) and the response to these circumstances by a range of social groups (who become variously involved in distribution, consumption, care and control).

The questions for us now are, to what extent can the responses of social groups develop in ways that decrease heroin problems whilst circumstances in society remain broadly the same, and to what extent must further improvements wait upon wider economic and political changes? Our answers will be cautiously optimistic where warranted but we shall be clear where we see no substantial prospects for improvement.

At the outset we can identify one sense in which certain manifestations of the heroin problem, if not its underlying dynamic, may be reduced in the coming years. If present trends in Britain are any indication then the spotlight of public attention may become partially redirected onto fresh issues of social concern – such as cocaine and other drugs (in ever more terrifying forms than have yet been dreamed of!); AIDS; alleged left-wing bias in the media; politicisation of the Church, or whatever. We do not mean to be particularly flippant here, merely to observe that as far as 'news values' and public interest go, social problems seem to have a finite life, after which they sink from view (although they may metamorphose or return to view after an absence). Continual repetition of the same sort of information and images is boring both for producers and consumers: only those members of the public who are caught up in the problem first hand are likely to wish to converse about it continuously and even they are likely to need some light relief.

It is therefore quite possible for a social problem to persist or to be still increasing in terms of persons directly involved or affected whilst, at the same time, it apparently fades or moves to one side in the priorities of the general population and public policy. This happened, for example, in the case of housing for low-income families in Britain in the 1970s. It is likely that society's perception of heroin problems will follow suit in the late 1980s. Enforcement measures being pursued nationally and internationally (described by Gerry Stimson in Chapter 2) may cause variations in supply between and within countries and from year to year, but are most unlikely to extinguish the trade. The persistence of social deprivation in many localities will continue to encourage small-scale distribution, to magnify the negative consequences of heroin consumption and to undermine community and professional responses, as Geoffrey Pearson describes in Chapter 3, on the basis of his recent research. Susanne MacGregor and Betsy Ettorre describe in Chapter 5 the slow history of progress towards making services socially as well as medically appropriate and towards expanding the services to meet the level of need. What are the chances of any government wanting to move any faster? No government is likely to want to see the problem defined in ways that make it appear to be first and foremost *its* responsibility – the fiscal costs are high, as are the political risks of failure. Hence this problem, together with others of an intractable nature, will be largely given back to the people to take 'their share' of responsibility and to solve or accommodate. This seems likely whichever political party is in power, although the ways in which the problem is defined or is offered may vary slightly.

The stances of the political parties

There are several standard, 'off the peg' political perspectives that can be identified as being on offer.

For the truly radical right, the best solution would be a free-market solution – legalise the product, save expenditure currently wasted on inefficient enforcement and make people responsible for their own private health care if they choose to get into trouble with drugs. It is notable however that at present such true free-market radicalism seems beyond the ambitions of any right-wing Western government, partly perhaps because of commitments entered into by the right in the 1960s in opposing the legalisation of drugs such as cannabis (a proposal then associated with sections of the liberal centre and left). Today the right is compromised by its commitments to law enforcement against drugs and support for parental anti-drug responses – commitments that it would have to rescind before taking any steps toward a full-blown market solution. In addition, the right (like other political positions) is committed to supporting international conventions aimed at the suppression of the trade, not its liberalisation. Here then, as in some other policy areas, the right is somewhat hamstrung by contradictory commitments.

For those in the social democratic centre of the political spectrum in Europe (roughly equivalent to the left of the mainstream spectrum in the USA), the causes of the drug problem are seen to lie in the processes of disruption and dissolution of political consensus, economic prosperity, social integration and community spirit which characterised earlier post-war years. The policies of the right (or, alternatively, the conflict between left and right) are blamed for the disruption of these tranquil conditions – and hence for heroin and other social problems arising in the 1980s. There is something to be said for this view insofar as heroin and other drug problems were certainly less severe twenty, or even ten, years ago. Correlation, however, does not establish cause: the nostalgic vision of earlier decades as devoid of social conflicts and anomie can well be queried, as can the proposition that the spread of heroin problems could have been checked by a society characterised by closer community ties. Even if the analysis of the centre were to be correct, there is still the problem that no government could turn back the clock; the readoption of policies followed in earlier years would not have the same effects in today's changed conditions. For example, there is undoubtedly a pressing need for greater expenditure on health and welfare services (as well as for the democratisation of those services and for greater choice and control over the form of provision regardless of one's ability to pay). But it is difficult to see in what ways more health and welfare services for users of heroin and other drugs can be more than a palliative or 'sponge', mopping up in the middle of a downpour. Greater public expenditure on other aspects of the 'social wage', particularly on housing and on employment generating measures, would help to decrease the proportion of people in areas of ready availability of heroin who suffer debilitating consequences (see Chapter 3). Yet it must also be remembered that even in more privileged material conditions people come to harm through use of heroin and other drugs, as we noted in the Introduction in relation to middle- and upper-class use. A comprehensive policy on heroin must therefore address not only the circumstances that push up the proportion of users who become seriously harmed, but must also address the problem of the widespread, ready availability of the drug. The political centre has no distinctive strategy in this respect.

What is striking about the situation in both Europe and the USA is the pre-emptive capture by the right of the moral high ground as well as of practical and policy recommendations. In the USA, Democrats fall over Republicans in their eagerness to declare themselves allied to the anti-drug movement, and this spectacle is enlivened further by calls from various quarters for the imposition of the death penalty for suppliers of drugs (*Narcotics Control Digest*, 1986, p. 1). In Britain, there is what passes as bipartisan agreement between Parliamentary right and left. But in reality what are shared are largely the propositions of the right, expressed in the language of the right. Labour Party spokespersons, including those on the left of the party, have supported legislation providing for yet higher penalties for traffickers and routinely join in calls for more customs officers (the 'Fortress Britain' approach) and for more vigorous enforcement measures in Third World countries. In the context of such commitments it is possible for left-wing politicians to sympathise with the plight of drug users and of their parents and communities in a quite general way and to call for enforcement, treatment and welfare responses to be better resourced. But the left finds it difficult to formulate a distinct and coherent view about the ways in which responses at personal, family, community, national and international levels should be organised. Having no distinctive drug policies of their own, the left is currently unable to give a lead in relation to this area – just as it was previously unable to give a lead in relation to the broader question of crime (Taylor, 1981; Lea and Young, 1984), where the right has also made the running (cf. Hall *et al.*, 1978).

Now there are no doubt, those who would feel that the low level of overt politicisation of heroin and other drug problems in the 1980s (following the rout of the liberal or 'permissive' viewpoint by the right in the 1960s) is a blessing, and that keeping political debate out of the area is a precondition for pragmatic, solution-oriented cooperation among all concerned. Whilst acknowledging the merit of this sentiment we also feel that more powerful solutions are required than are at present being implemented and that a greater degree of informed political debate could play a role in clarifying the options. Certainly, the present consensus on the problem, as witnessed by politicians and public figures simply jumping on the anti-drug bandwagon, is not getting us much nearer workable solutions. The discourse of anti-drug policy, as crystallised in certain key sloganised propositions – such as 'Just Say No' (personal choice) and 'Stopping Supply at Source' (change the Third World not our society) – simply does not articulate a reasonable range of policy options. A more sophisticated (one might say less simple-minded) level of debate is necessary. When saying this we do not propose the exclusion of the supposedly non-sophisticated, 'ordinary' lay person, such as parents of drug users (or users themselves), from debate. Indeed, quite the contrary, for those currently tackling the problem at grassroots level are, at the very least, as sophisticated in their thinking as the politicians at national level (and indeed, perhaps more so).

A framework for policy at local, national and international levels

Let us turn then, to some of the considerations that are effectively disregarded or suppressed in the national debate. We propose that a framework for generating options for restraining and possibly reducing heroin-related problems can be generated by drawing upon two sources – on the one hand, the kinds of policy analysis and findings from research presented in this book and, on the other hand, the experiences of practitioners (both lay and professional) who are responding to the problem.

In respect of the policy analysis side, we propose that some version of the model of the problem presented in the Introduction to this collection can serve as a point of departure. (Readers may find it useful to refer back to the diagram on page 4 of the Introduction at this point.) Summarising, this model identifies three broad levels of the problem: 'grassroots', national and international. In the following paragraphs we appraise the possibilities for success at each of these three levels. First we look at the grassroots level of social groups responding, where there are some encouraging directions of development. Next we look at the drug problem in the context of the national economy, where the possibilities are less immediate but nonetheless provocative. Finally we turn to the international level – in particular to the subject of crop substitution in the context of development programmes – where past experience has not been encouraging (but see Stimson's chapter in this volume).

Grassroots strategies: learning from experience

The experiences and perspectives of practitioners – professionals, community activists, parents of users, and so on – provide a touchstone for interpreting and evaluating policy ideas about responses at the local, community or grassroots level. In several of the preceding chapters (particularly those by Pearson and by Donoghoe *et al.*) emphasis has been placed upon lay responses. It is also, of course, necessary and useful to refer to the perspectives of professionals working in the drug field. To help to elucidate some of these perspectives – as espoused by the 'mainstream' professionals in the field – we shall refer to the reports of the Advisory Council on Misuse of Drugs (to which reference is also made by MacGregor and Ettorre in this volume). The Advisory Council is a committee of doctors, social workers, education professionals and others appointed by the Home Office Secretary of State to advise the

British government on the drug problem and what to do about it. What influence the ACMD may have had in previous years has been largely overshadowed by the creation of a Ministerial Group in 1984. However, the reports of the Council, in particular *Treatment and Rehabilitation* (1982) and *Prevention* (1984), still stand as expressions of the concerns of a range of practitioners in the drugs field. In particular, the Council's articulation of concepts such as the 'problem drug user' and 'reducing the harm associated with drug misuse', as practical and legitimate goals of policy (alongside the more generally understood goal of reduction in levels of consumption) reflects much of what doctors, social workers, parents and others *actually do* on a day-to-day basis.

Originally, for example, the 'British system' of prescribing opiates to persons who had become dependent on heroin was seen as a legitimate way of maintaining their ability to lead 'a useful and fairly normal way of life' (Ministry of Health, 1926, p. 32). Today, long-term prescription of synthetic opiate substitutes such as methadone has fallen out of psychiatric fashion (and prescription of heroin even more so), but the idea behind the practice is still widely understood. Harm-reduction strategies are also the daily practice of many youth workers, particularly in detached settings where the practical opportunities for preventing drug use are limited. However, lest it be thought that it is only woolly-headed, over-liberal or permissive young professionals who practise harm-reduction, let us also note the involvement of the police and of parents in these strategies. It is, for example, quite widely accepted amongst drug-squad officers that it makes no sense to 'bust' all accessible users; the priority given to catching the dealers implies a *de facto* partial decriminalisation of drug use itself, and the development of a more sympathetic, almost 'welfarist' perspective upon the user and her or his needs. What the police sometimes describe as their 'welfare' or 'community' roles can, of course, also mask or try to excuse intrusive and disruptive policing strategies (particularly against ethnic and other minorities), but the 'welfare' aspect can carry an element of truth. In the drugs field this can involve giving useful and sympathetic advice and assistance in contacting social services and/or specialist treatment agencies. More striking than these accommodations by the police are some of the harm-reduction strategies which parents of users can find themselves adopting.

We shall be going into more detail about such harm-reduction strategies in subsequent paragraphs. What we wish to register here is that virtually all professional and lay persons who have anything to do with drug users find themselves adopting some aspects of harm-reduction strategies at some time or another – in spite of the fact that most are firmly opposed to such strategies in principle (because harm-reduction is seen by many as condoning drug use). Even quite vehement opposition in principle seems no bar to adopting practical harm-reduction solutions in specific circumstances (as indeed, for example, in the actions of some perplexed parents, cf. Chapter 4 by Donoghoe *et al.*).

Now it is possible to take one of two views on this mismatch of theory and practice. Either one can say that this is a potentially embarrassing inconsistency that is best left undisturbed, or one can say that here is something important to understand and push forward into the policy spotlight. Whilst we have some sympathy with the former view, we cleave to the latter.

Our sympathy for the 'keep quiet' view is based on our appreciation that some practitioners may be made to feel vulnerable and may find their practice under close and unwelcome scrutiny if it becomes suspected that they are in any way 'colluding' with the drug user. The defence that 'one was trying to help reduce the harm to the user' may not prevent the practitioner (lay or professional) being criticised by neighbours or colleagues, suspended or otherwise disciplined by management, or pilloried in the local media. After all, drug use remains an illegal, potentially dangerous and consensually immoral activity, and the only really safe strategy for practitioners is to dissociate themselves from it in every possible way. Many practitioners would not welcome too close an enquiry into what they actually do in relation to drug users, precisely because they are aware that their repertoire of responses includes the publicly unacceptable harm-reduction approach and this is best continued quietly rather than flaunted publicly. Simply to raise the issue of harm-minimisation then, is to place many practitioners at risk.

It is, therefore, with an awareness of the risks involved that we support the view that the issue of harm-reduction should be placed firmly in the spotlight. We think this because we believe that the continuing marginalisation of harm-reduction strategies – we could go further and speak of the suppression of hard-won and practical information about how to help people who need help – is itself a cause of unnecessary and unjustifiable distress for both drug users and those who seek to help them. If the public silence on harm-reduction could be breached, then both users and helpers could more easily develop ways of alleviating drug-related problems, instead of individuals and small groups having to 'reinvent the wheel' in isolation, confusion and shame.

In order to win the argument about harm-reduction, two things are necessary. First, one must make clear that one is not attempting to substitute harm-reduction for use-reduction as the preventive goal; rather, each is complementary to the other. Let us state this clearly. If strategies to reduce harm can be implemented in a more general and effective way than is currently the case, and if these can be supplemented by only slightly more effective strategies to reduce levels of use (see next section), then the joint effect would be a worthwhile reduction in the problem overall. The second thing that is necessary to win the argument is to illustrate clearly, what harm-reduction actually is; at present, the debate over principle has run ahead of descriptions of the practice.

Let us, then, explore the practical possibilities for harm-reduction, seeing these as adjuncts rather than alternatives to strategies to reduce availability and consumption. What are the varieties of 'harm' (to use the language of the ACMD *Prevention* report) or of 'problems' (in the terminology of the *Treatment and Rehabilitation* report) that practitioners observe in relation to heroin – and in what ways do they act to reduce those problems?

These are not solely physical or psychological problems, but also social and environmental problems. A multiple drug user may have a range of problems, being concurrently psychologically dependent on some drugs and physiologically dependent on others, and at the same time having financial or legal problems or difficulties over housing. The response to the needs of the drug user therefore requires a fully multi-disciplinary approach. This approach should be problem-orientated rather than specifically client or substance orientated. It would be similar to that in the field of alcohol where the term problem drinker has been defined by the Advisory Council on Alcoholism. Thus a problem drug taker would be any person who experiences social, psychological, physical or legal problems related to intoxication and/or regular excessive consumption and/or as a consequence of his [*sic*] own use of drugs . . . each element produces its own specific social, medical and legal problems and separating these out can aid planning of individual treatments and relevant services (ACMD, 1982, p. 34).

The ACMD went on to describe 'a framework of services for the future' in which Regional Drug Problem Teams, headed by 'a consultant psychiatrist (specialising in drug problems) working not less than six sessions per week' would give leadership to District Drug Advisory Committees which would, in turn, encourage the development of services at a local level. It was perhaps unfortunate (though unsurprising from a historical point of view) that the Drug Dependency Unit (clinic) staff were given pride of place in this blueprint at the very time when this institution was recognised as being past its zenith and as not having adapted to the varied needs of drug users. Such a framework underplayed the contributions of non-statutory agencies, of generic services (statutory and non-statutory) and of lay, community and parental responses. The ACMD's interest in erecting a structure for coordination of services also distracted attention from the equally (some would say more) important question of practice – what exactly were the freshly-coordinated services supposed to be doing? Perhaps the attempt to shift the clinic into the community involved too much uncertainty for articulate descriptions to be possible. Perhaps, also, conflicts within the medical profession (between those clinic psychiatrists who still believed that maintenance prescribing still served a purpose and those who saw it as a form of collusion with the patient, and between psychiatrists and general practitioners, some of whom were suspected of over-generous prescribing), and conflicts and resentments between the medical and social workers in the non-statutory sector, made a spelling-out of clear thinking on practice more difficult. Certainly, the underrepresentation of the growing and relatively innovative non-statutory services on the ACMD, and the virtual exclusion of lay practitioners, stripped the 'framework' of much of its potential detail.

We can now, however, take up the opportunity of separating

the various aspects of drug-related problems – physical/medical, social/psychological and legal – and go on to identify some of the ways in which harm is reduced in each of these areas.

As far as *physical harm* is concerned, the two main areas of danger are life-threatening diseases conveyed by infections transmitted by needles shared between injecting users, and overdoses caused by using too high a dose of a drug or by use of more than one sedative drug contemporaneously. During the mid-1980s, a debate raged around the proposition that a ready supply of sterilised needles would reduce the sharing of needles and hence transmission of infection such as HIV (the AIDS virus, formerly called HTLV3) and hepatitis (itself a serious disease, but one that became somewhat overshadowed by AIDS in the 1980s). Those who opposed a ready supply of clean needles feared that non-injecting drug users (for example, those who inhale vapours or swallow pills) might be tempted to begin injecting their nostrum, or that existing injectors might be encouraged to continue doing so, yet not always be bothered to obtain fresh needles. Very obviously, if needles were altogether forsaken in favour of other modes of administration (such as inhalation, smoking and snorting) then cross-infection would not occur. A radical strategy for reduction of physical harm might involve public education on the relative dangers of different modes of administration, but so far there do not appear to be many advocates of such a strategy. In 1987, at least, most participants in the debate seemed to accept the persistence of the practice of hypodermic penetration of the body. An alternative perspective would allow the possibility of ways of gaining pleasure without such penetration (cf. the 'safe sex' debate). Would-be advocates of a 'safe use' strategy are to some extent hamstrung by the difficulties of communicating effectively with existing injectors without acknowledging the attractions of injection as seen by this group; without such acknowledgement, existing injectors might not feel sufficiently directly 'addressed', yet any such acknowledgement might be seen as advocacy of the very practice which it sought to contain. There are clear parallels here with the field of sexual politics. What is needed, we feel, is some way of ensuring that clean needles are available to those for whom hypodermic penetration is an essential act, but not foisted upon those for whom other means of administration, for example, smoking, are acceptable or preferable.

Overdoses are caused primarily by two conjunctions of circumstances: either high-dose sedative use (particularly dangerous with heroin if done after a period of abstention, during which the body becomes unaccustomed to previously-tolerated levels of the drug); or using more than one type of sedative drug in the same period of time. The mid-1980s saw several well-publicised cases of death that illustrate these dangers. Working-class teenager Jason Fitzsimmons died in 1985 in Merseyside of a high dose of the sedative Dalmane and of some possible interaction between the effects of this drug and of methadone and heroin taken previously ('Jason was not killed by Heroin', *Northern Echo*, 30 January 1986). In the following year, upper-middle-class student Olivia Channon died in a college of Oxford University after drinking alcohol and using heroin ('Party cocktail of heroin and alcohol killed Channon girl', *The Times*, 5 September 1986). However, in spite of the fact that such specific dangers have been known to experts for some time, the British government's anti-heroin campaigns for 1985–6 and 1986–7 played down potentially life-saving information about common causes of overdoses, preferring to make general statements about dangers of heroin *per se*. There is some way to go before Britain could claim to have a public information or education strategy concerned with the reduction of numbers of drug-related deaths.

Strategies for reduction of *social and personal harm* have been addressed in preceding chapters by Pearson and Donoghoe *et al*. Pearson drew attention to the importance of time-structuring for styles of involvement with heroin and other drugs. When people slip out of any correspondence with timetables imposed from outside, they find it more difficult to avoid slipping further into heavy involvement with drugs and the timetables of scoring, intoxication, socialising with other users, resting, scoring again (etc.) provided by the drug scene. This is well appreciated by social-work, advice and counselling agencies whose staff espouse the value of drug users 'keeping in touch' and getting involved in activities other than drug use. Part of the intention is to provide social and cultural involvements that may in the longer term serve as alternatives to drug use, but there is also the shorter-term aim of keeping the drug user relatively stable and involved in non-drug activities and relationships alongside their drug use; the person continues to be involved with drugs but to the exclusion of other things, and hence is helped to keep within broader social networks and to avoid becoming totally estranged. Many parents who have no formal knowledge of social-work practice find themselves adopting similar integrationist strategies, often after an initial period in which they reject the user. The aim is to rebuild the framework of family, support the user as 'one of us' and within this to conduct the longer-term struggle to root out drug use altogether (Dorn, Ribbens and South, 1987). Reduction of social harm – isolation, rejection, lack of options – is an essential ingredient in the practices of many other groups. Quite ambitious strategies to reduce social problems related to drug use can be seen in the community activism of local people in areas such as Tenantsrise (see Chapter 4), where it becomes understood that several interlinked aspects of the locality – poor housing, crippling levels of unemployment, lack of recreational facilities – combine to deepen what would otherwise be less pressing drug problems (cf. Chapter 3). In these circumstances, struggles for material resources to improve the social life of local people are inseparable from strategies to reduce drug problems.

As far as reduction of *legal problems* is concerned we can point to strategies developed by doctors, parents and police. The medical approach to reduction of drug-related legal problems has traditionally focused upon provision of opiate drugs under prescription. This had two aims: reduction of the possibility that an individual drug user might get involved in 'bad company' and in criminal acts in order to finance his or her purchases of drugs, and the attempt to contain or restrict the overall size of the illicit market which might, if left unchecked, recruit new users. Although opiate prescribing has largely fallen out of favour with drug clinic psychiatrists in Britain, some parents find themselves adopting a very similar strategy on occasions. So, for example, parents find themselves giving money to their children to purchase heroin, accompanying their children to the place where the dealing is done, even going and getting the drug themselves and bringing it home – all in order to curtail their children's contacts with the illicit market and to reduce the possibilities that the son or daughter will go thieving in order to finance drug purchases. In the circumstances of expansion of the availability of heroin well beyond the capacity or indeed willingness of the clinic system to provide a licit supply, some parents take up this role (albeit to obtain illegal supplies) – and suffer probably far more of the same ambivalence, as well as laying themselves open to legal repercussions.

While talking of reduction of legal harm it is necessary to refer to recent legislative changes in relation to offences of supply. During the post-war period, there has been an increasing tendency to distinguish between the drug user as 'victim' and the supplier as 'corruptor' (Young, 1973). Acts of Parliament did not at first distinguish between penalties for possession and for supply, but then provided for heavier penalties for supply (and 'possession with intent to supply') and subsequently widened the gap. By the mid-1980s, supply of drugs in large amounts was defined as a major crime and penalties extended to life imprisonment without prospect of parole, and confiscation of all assets which the convicted person could not show to be derived from legal means. The question of whether or not such penalties are effective, and if so, how, has been obscured by populist rhetoric about the fight against a new (or rediscovered) folk-devil, the pusher. It is worth bearing in mind, even at risk of being thought to be soft on the drugs issue, that increases in penalty in the past have not been notably successful in reducing the problem; there is little reason to think that the latest penalties (life sentences and forfeiture of assets – as high as we can go short of the death penalty) will fare any better. Indeed successive penalty increases may worsen the situation in one respect, since they frighten the amateurs out of the trade and create an enlarged role for the tightly organised and security-conscious criminal firm. Routine or casual exchange of drugs between users at a local level continues, but few people would wish to be involved in the middle or upper ranks of distribution unless heavily-enough involved to make the risks worthwhile. One consequence is the development of the drug distribution business in forms very resistant to penetration by law enforcement agents; we have a combination of high penalties in theory and virtually no penalty in practice for the big supplier. Our moral outrage, when converted into legal form, has not exactly created the figure of the pusher; but it is fair enough to say that we have provided the environment in which he or she flourishes. In this respect the development of legal control has done little to reduce the problem, and alternative approaches need to be examined.

Innovative national or local strategies to reduce drug distribution

In Chapter 3, Pearson refers to research into the spread of heroin in localities suffering from multiple deprivation. Elsewhere, and in a more general way, we ourselves have attempted to describe the way in which the expansion of the *irregular economy* constructs the conduits running throughout the regions and neighbourhoods of Britain within which the distribution of drugs occurs (Auld *et al.*, 1986). We suggest that it is within the context of a degree of involvement in this irregular economy that the bulk of heroin distribution is currently taking place – not all of it in deprived localities, as Pearson of course acknowledges.

The irregular economy in work, goods and services is an integral part of the general or 'regular' (licit) economy of a country (Ferman and Ferman, 1973). It expands in periods of economic restructuring, recession and unemployment, when conditions do not favour persons' (for example, young people's) entry into the mainstream of the regular economy, as well as in periods of affluence when certain goods or services are scarce. The irregular economy provides multiple conduits for the distribution and exchange of drugs alongside a variety of other goods and services, prostitution, the disposal of stolen goods, and so on. In relation to heroin and other drugs, the more comprehensive distribution system (i) connects with a greater number of potential consumers and, (ii) sucks in supplies. It follows that there are two possibilities for control:

1. reduction of the total size and scope of the irregular economy of which drug distribution is a part;
2. reduction of the extent of drug distribution within the irregular economy by (for example) displacing drug distribution by other activities that currently form a part of the irregular economy.

These possibilities may be summarised as displacing the irregular economy *per se*, and/or replacing its drug-related parts by non-drug (but still irregular) alternative activities. The question then arises, how might these be achieved?

Strategies aiming to shift drug distributors into other activities within the irregular economy

Generalising, we suggest that expansion of the irregular economy occurs when pre-existing structures of economic activity and opportunity are disrupted by economic change and become inadequate to integrate wide sections of the population who thereby become economically and socially 'marginal'. Some groups turn to petty criminal activities as a means of supplementing licit incomes and also to 'have something to do' – as a way of life (cf. Bales, 1984; also Chapter 3, this volume). There are, in addition, links between the various parts of the irregular economy, and these links can be observed in particular sectors, for example, links between international banking, 'loansharking', drug distribution (RCMP, 1983), government (Rose, 1984) and police corruption (Rottenburg, 1968).

Thus the illegal business of drug distribution has links 'downwards' into relatively powerless and economically marginal groups in society, and 'upwards' into systems of law enforcement, government (in some cases) and finance. Ferreting out these links and designing selective and effective countermeasures are obviously not simple matters. However, some existing and planned control activities of government and law enforcement agencies are relevant and potentially useful in restricting drug-related aspects of the irregular economy.

For example, taking a cue from the legal codes of the USA and other countries, the British Parliament has recently passed legislation designed to relieve any person convicted of drug trafficking of the whole of that person's assets, unless he or she can show that part or all of the assets was obtained by legal means (Drugs Trafficking Offences Act). There have also been intermittent reports that the British tax authorities are following (or experimenting with) the American strategy of assessing income tax of suspected dealers on the basis of their assumed illegal incomes. Such interventions, if vigorously pursued in respect of persons suspected or proved to be involved in drug importation and major distribution, may have some impact upon these activities, with the possible result that such persons will shift over to other, less-risky irregular activities (or even become honest citizens). These measures do not however have much bearing upon the lowest levels of the drug distribution system (let us say from regional 'wholesaler' downwards), since the amount of work required to build a case for forfeiture of assets or for swingeing tax assessment would be disproportionately large in comparison with the numbers of small dealers and the relatively low level of their assets.[1] Forfeiture and tax claims are, then, tactics to be tried out against the big operators.

It might perhaps also be possible to develop economic inducements to major drug suppliers to move into other areas of the irregular (or even regular) economy; such inducements would include strategies for increasing their expectations of the costs of drug distribution and for decreasing their perceptions of the likely benefits (Rottenberg, 1968).

It is sometimes suggested that a legal system of drug distribution would undercut the illegal markets (or at least the upper parts of that market; one might still have a degree of improper passing-on of drugs at lower, local levels). Whatever one's assessment of the effects of this suggestion, it is, as we observed earlier, almost certainly not politically feasible under any conceivable British administration other than perhaps one that eschewed commitments to suppress the drugs trade and instead took a theory of 'self-regulating' markets more literally than do the present British or other Western governments.

It is however, worth considering the possibility of reducing (only partially) the levels of criminal penalties for major drug offences (although we do not propose this). Some economic and criminological assessments suggest that the degree of monopolisation and the levels of profit encouraged by very heavy sentences have the result of 'hardening' criminal drug-dealing enterprises against intervention by law enforcement agencies, and that the threat of heavy sentences thereby consolidates a nigh-impregnable system of supply; only the amateurs, couriers and low-level operatives are open to being apprehended. According to this argument, a reduction in penalties might open up the trade to more competition and also to law enforcement. Such an argument would however be difficult to put in the political forum, and it must be made clear that its prophetic validity is open to question. An alternative point of view is that whilst the historical increase in severity of penalties for drug importation and distribution may have contributed to the impregnability of the trade, any decrease of penalties today would not restore the situation to what it was. We have some sympathy with this view, believing (i) that only a very great reduction in penalties would be effective in opening up established monopoly criminal structures to effective competition, changing those structures in ways that make law enforcement more effective; and (ii) that inducements at middle and lower levels of the distribution system would remain, thus still sucking in drug imports, albeit by different routes than those of today. On balance, we think that it is at least worth considering the argument for decreases in penalties for drug distribution, acknowledging that this is an argument that could not be won at the present time; and we see absolutely nothing to be gained from yet further increases in penalties.

We have been writing so far of the major dealer (importer, wholesaler, regional distributor, etc.). Turning now to the lower-level dealer and the user-dealer, let us ask what strategies might shift the activities of these persons away from drug-related towards non-drug-related aspects of the irregular economy.

As far as user-dealers are concerned, the British experience of Drug Dependency Units and of some post-war drug research is relevant. One of the hopes pinned to the British 'clinic system' in the late 1960s was that a user who could obtain his or her nostrum from licit sources would not need to enter the illegal market. It became clear however that some users would sell part of their clinic supplies – perhaps because they had been prescribed too much, or because they preferred to obtain some other drugs available in the market, or because they wished to raise income for other purposes, or because such sale and the social contacts around the small-scale illicit market were valued parts of their preferred life-styles. The clinics today have few patients on long-term maintenance, and generally restrict new patients to a short course of decreasing dosage, or offer social casework without drugs. Whether or not 'throwing heroin at the problem' would help to reduce today's users' involvements with the irregular economy is a matter of contention in Britain today. It is not easy to see what alternative activities within the irregular economy would appeal to drug users, but certainly withdrawal from a drug-using life-style would have to take account of the kinds of problems and issues raised in Chapter 3.

Strategies aiming to reduce the overall size of the irregular economy and hence reduce its drug-distribution-related aspects

We turn now to strategies for undermining the broader irregular economy of which drug importing, distribution and dealing form part. It is of course possible that reduction in the size of the irregular economy overall could coexist with a compensatory expansion of its drug-related aspects, but we shall ignore that possibility for the time being, and assume that a reduction in the irregular economy would tend to reduce drug distribution.

One obvious way to attempt to reduce the irregular economy (at both 'top' and 'bottom' ends of the market, that is, from shady financing and business deals to petty crime and rip-offs), would be to reverse the social and economic conditions that encourage its expansion. Since economic and demographic restructuring and changes which do not generate opportunities for regular work for the population groups concerned are among the causes of the growth of the irregular economy in Western countries, it follows that the options for the future include (i) a reversal or slowing down of economic and consequent demographic and social changes, with some kind of management of those changes so that more 'regular' jobs and opportunities are made available than would otherwise be the case; and/or (ii) employment training and community regeneration approaches with displaced population groups so as to encourage them to adapt to current conditions other than opportunities for involvement in the irregular economy.

Such structural and social strategies – aiming to reduce the general conditions (summarised here as 'the irregular economy') within which a range of anti-social activities including drug distribution flourish – are likely to be more effective than any approach that ignores the conditions generating crime and that relies purely upon enforcement measures to deter people from taking advantage of the opportunities that arise in those conditions. As the recent British Crime Survey observed, 'a substantial body of research indicates that it is difficult to enhance the police effect on crime . . . In particular, it is becoming clear that the effectiveness of the "core" of policing – preventive patrol, and investigation – cannot be sufficiently improved by increased manning levels' (Hough and Mayhew, 1983, p. 34). If the irregular economy retains its present scope or slightly expands in Britain, then the balance will tip further away from law-enforcement agencies whatever staffing levels are achieved, since so many people will be involved in aspects of the irregular economy as to reduce public cooperation with the police against those activities. People are unlikely to act against what they perceive to be the interests of themselves, their associates, neighbours and family.

Summarising, we can suggest that economic policies aiming to encourage participation in the regular economy and hence shift people away from involvement with the irregular economy (including involvement with drug distribution) may be necessary (if not sufficient) conditions for more effective drug control. Cooperation between those formulating and implementing local economic policy, health and welfare services and policing would be a prerequisite of trying out innovative prevention strategies on a local or regional level. There is obviously scope for experimenting with a range of imaginative control schemes in some localities at least, carefully evaluating processes of implementation and outcomes, as suggested by Stimson in Chapter 2. Having said that, we can add that serious evaluation of current policies seems to be almost entirely lacking; a comparative approach would be most useful, given our current state of ignorance.

Contradictions at the international level: tackling the problem at source?

As regards the international level, the most apparently obvious policy would be to continue to attempt to stem the flow of heroin supply by mounting a greater number of carefully planned and well-resourced agricultural development projects in Third World countries.

It seems to be generally understood that, even in those cases where a Third World government may agree to opt for apparently more decisive measures such as burning or spraying crops or taking severely punitive actions against farmers, such measures often simply delay or displace cropping. What is becoming more apparent now, however, is that even the 'velvet glove' approach of development projects may have these same effects. Better transportation is introduced, yield-increasing inputs such as fertilisers are made more generally available, the cash economy is broadened, yet each development project has only a limited life after which its benefits often run down. What can happen is that poppy-growing shifts to adjoining areas during the life of the development project, then steals back as alternative benefits and close surveillance run down. At the beginning of each planting season, agents of merchants visit the farmers, offering good-quality seeds and a hefty cash advance on the crop – sometimes with the assurance that if the authorities destroy the crop then the advance will not need to be repaid. The benefits to the merchant are considerable and he can well afford to bargain that the majority of the crop planted will accrue to him if at least part of the growing cycle escapes the attention of the authorities, since by then the farmer is committed to this crop for the support of his family and can be counted upon to resist any attempt to destroy the growing crop.[2] Only a government which makes no attempt to rule by consent can destroy crops in more than a limited and exemplary, showpiece manner.

In one sense then, agricultural development projects may even consolidate poppy production in the longer term, since they enhance the penetration of market relations and increase the expectations of farmers, whilst providing really distracting alternatives to poppy cultivation only in the short term. Meanwhile, a similar outcome occurs in relation to enforcement efforts against the illicit 'kitchen' laboratories in which opium is converted to heroin. Some laboratories are closed down, perhaps some arrests made, but the conversion process simply shifts to another site, and may return when jeeps, helicopters and foreign advisers move on. Even if one looks at the issues only from a financial point of view, ignoring the politics and ethics of the situation, it is evident that it is not possible to turn all areas capable of growing opium poppy into military zones on a continuous basis, whilst periodic changes in enforcement responses simply shift the problem about and may expand it.

The situation is further complicated by the historical observation that development programmes of crop substitution and/or eradication seem generally to have been tied up with other political strategies of the donor (grant-giving) countries (Simmons and Said, 1974). In the 1970s the production of heroin for international trade occurred mainly in the 'Golden Triangle' of the Far East, which was also the site of anti-Communist and anti-National Liberation struggles sponsored by Western countries, principally the USA. There is evidence that whilst one arm of US foreign policy was working to eradicate opium and heroin production, the other arm was forming political and economic alliances with local anti-Communist groups heavily involved in the opium trade; McCoy *et al.* (1972) have documented aspects of this in the Golden Triangle. Later, in the 1980s the West was giving support to anti-Communist (particularly Afghan) elements in the 'Golden Crescent' around the north-western borders of Pakistan. One consequence of these alliances and the 'open border' thereby created, was that opium (and possibly heroin) produced in the north gained easy access into Pakistan. Even if one does not take too literally Pakistan's recent claims to be succeeding in reducing domestic poppy production, it is difficult to dismiss her observations that the flow of opium into the country from her neighbours has increased, with consequences not only for her heroin export to the West but also for increased availability and consumption inside Pakistan (PNCB, 1986).

One does not have to adopt a 'conspiracy theory' and say that any Western agency is encouraging the heroin trade as a matter of policy. One can simply acknowledge unintended consequences of complicated alliances within an unsettled region. It is undoubtedly the case that there is a great deal more at stake in the region than drug supply. As one analyst puts it:

Popular perception in Pakistan holds that the American policy on Afghanistan is to bleed the Russians to the last Afghan. On a more sophisticated level, however, most of the existing views in this vein can be seen from the following . . . levels. On the local (Afghan) level, the US policy aims at making Afghanistan a Vietnam for Moscow . . . On the regional level, the US policy aims at putting Moscow on the defensive, embarrassing it . . . in the words of a leading American official Sovietologist, 'We never got the Russians so cheap'. On the East–West level, the US policy aims at using the Afghan card as a *quid pro quo* on some regional issues . . . [and hopes that] by keeping the Soviet southern border 'hot', the Soviet Muslim population would eventually get 'contaminated', making Moscow an unstable and inward-looking state in future years (Tauqueer Shiekh, 1986, p. 4).

If these observations carry any weight, then one can see the possibility that 'national security' considerations of a regional and global nature are sufficiently to the fore for any potential backwash in terms of heroin supply to be recognised and implicitly accepted. It is often asserted by control agencies that the international channels for supply of weapons and of drugs largely overlap: this certainly appears to be the case in relation to the 'Golden Crescent', where the borders of Pakistan, Iran and Afghanistan meet. If part of the price of keeping the underbelly of the USSR 'hot' is the compromise of anti-narcotics goals, then we should not be surprised to find that price being paid.

On balance then, development programmes and linked enforcement strategies in Third World regions can be seen to be less effective in reducing supply than might initially be supposed, and further undermined by other regional policies of Western powers. Development programmes may have much to be said for them (and much to be critically said against them) on other grounds but they are of limited effectiveness in reducing the supply of heroin. To effect a lasting reduction of availability within Western (and Eastern) countries, we shall have to look elsewhere. The rhetoric of 'tackling the problem at source' may have more of a distracting effect on policy formation than on poppy cultivation.

*   *   *

In conclusion, we propose that the strategy of tackling the problem 'at source' is deeply flawed as long as the source of our problems is seen as being in the Third World. In a sensible world, crop substitution in the context of development programmes might work well. In present circumstances, Western countries concerned about heroin should look for solutions closer to home – in their economic, social and criminological policies. This chapter has attempted to summarise some of the options for reducing drug availability by reducing drug distribution within the broader irregular economy. We have also drawn to the reader's attention some of the ways in which a variety of practitioners (professionals, lay volunteers and parents) practise harm-reduction in relation to physical, social and legal problems related to drugs. The best way forward, we suggest, would involve innovative economic and criminological strategies to restrain availability, together with consolidation and extension of practitioners' existing strategies to minimise harm associated with consumption.

Notes

1. There is anxiety in some quarters that although the forfeiture legislation is intended to be used primarily against those 'high up' in trafficking organisations, the difficulties of bringing such people to court and obtaining a conviction for trafficking (which is a necessary prerequisite of forfeiture) may cause the police to settle for forfeiture action against middle- and lower-level dealers (Goodsir, 1986). Against this it may be said that such a general trend does not appear to have occurred in the USA where such legislation has been in place for some time; indeed there seem to be difficulties in giving law enforcement greater 'bite' at any level of drug distribution. Problems relating to the higher levels include difficulties in getting bank disclosure rules to work and persistent failures of inter-agency cooperation (Select Committee on Narcotics Abuse and Control, 1977; Comptroller General, 1979; US General Accounting Office, 1985).
2. Comment based upon conversations between the first author and a number of informed observers during two visits to Pakistan in 1986.

Bibliography

Aberle, D. and Naegele, K. (1968) 'Middle-class Fathers' Occupational Role and Attitude towards Children', in Bell and Vogel (1968).

Advisory Committee on Drug Dependence (1968) *The Rehabilitation of Drug Addicts* (London: HMSO).

Advisory Council on the Misuse of Drugs (1980) *Report on Drug Dependents within the Prison System in England and Wales* (London: Home Office).

Advisory Council on the Misuse of Drugs (1982) *Treatment and Rehabilitation* (London: HMSO).

Advisory Council on the Misuse of Drugs (1984) *Prevention* (London: HMSO).

Agar, M. (1973) *Ripping and Running: A Formal Ethnography of Urban Heroin Addicts* (New York: Seminar Press).

Anonymous (1967) 'Measures against Drug Addiction', *British Medical Journal*, 11 February. pp. 319–20.

Auld, J., Dorn, N. and South, N. (1984/5) 'Heroin Now: Bringing It All Back Home', *Youth and Policy*, 9, Summer, pp. 1–7.

Auld, J., Dorn, N. and South, N. (1986) 'Irregular Work, Irregular Pleasures: Heroin in the 1980s', in Matthews, R. and Young, J. (eds) *Confronting Crime* (London: Sage).

Backett, K. (1982) *Mothers and Fathers: A Study of the Development and Negotiation of Parental Behaviour* (London: Macmillan).

Baden, A. (1972) 'Homicide, Suicide and Accidental Death among Narcotic Addicts', *Human Pathology*, 3, pp. 91–5.

Badinter, E. (1981) *The Myth of Motherhood: An Historical View of the Maternal Instinct* (London: Souvenir Press).

Bakke, E. (1968) 'The Cycle of Adjustment to Unemployment', in Bell and Vogel (1968).

Bales, K. (1984) 'The Dual Labour Market of the Criminal Economy' in Collins, R. (ed.) *Sociological Theory* (London: Jossey Bass).

Bell, N. and Vogel, E. (eds) (1968) *A Modern Introduction to the Family* (London: Collier Macmillan).

Bennett, T. and Wright, R. (1985) *Burglars on Burglary* (Aldershot: Gower).

Bennett, T. and Wright, R. (1986) 'The Drug-taking Careers of Opioid Users', *Howard Journal of Criminal Justice*, 25, p. 1.

Berridge, V. (1984) 'Drugs and Social Policy: The Establishment of Drug Control in Britain 1900–1930', *British Journal of Addiction*, 79, pp. 17–29.

Berridge, V. and Edwards, G. (1981) *Opium and the People* (London: Allen Lane).

Bill, L. (1980) *Tough Love: Alternative to Enabling* (London: Families Anonymous).

Blackwell, J. (1984) 'Drifting, Controlling and Overcoming: Opiate Users who Avoid Becoming Chronically Dependent', *Journal of Drug Issues*, 13, p. 2.

Blenheim Project (1983) *How to Stop: A Do-it-yourself Guide to Opiate Withdrawal* (London: Blenheim Project).

Bosworth-Davies, R. (1985) 'Drugs: Looking for Mr *X*', *Police Review*, 93, p. 2164.

Boulton, M. (1983) *On Being a Mother: A Study of Women and Pre-school Children* (London: Tavistock Publications).

Bourdieu, P. and Passeron, J. (1977) *Reproduction* (London: Sage).

British Medical Journal (1986) 'Editorial: Government Hypocrisy on Drugs', *British Medical Journal*, 292, p. 712.

Brown, G. and Harris, T. (1978) *Social Origins of Depression* (London: Tavistock).

Bulletin on Narcotics (1984) 'Editorial Note', 36, 4, p. 1.

Bulmer, M. (1986) *Neighbours: The Work of Phillip Abrams* (Cambridge: Cambridge University Press).

Campbell, R. (1984) *Overdose Aid: A Simple Guide to Coping with Drug-induced Crises* (Manchester: Lifeline Project).

Central Office of Information (1978) *The Prevention and Treatment of Drug Misuse in Britain* (London: HMSO).

Chain, I., Gerard, D., Lee, R. and Rosenfeld, E. (1964) *Narcotics, Delinquency and Social Policy: The Road to H* (London: Tavistock).

Chodorow, N. (1978) *The Reproduction of Mothering: Psychoanalysis and the Sociology of Gender* (California: University of California Press).

Cloward, R. and Ohlin, L. (1960) *Delinquency and Opportunity* (New York: Free Press).

Cohen, S. (1980) *Folk Devils and Moral Panics* (Oxford: Martin Robertson).

Coleman, A. (1985) *Utopia on Trial: Vision and Reality in Planned Housing* (London: Hilary Shipman).

Comptroller General (1979) *Gains Made in Controlling Illegal Drugs, Yet the Drug Trade Flourishes*, Report to the Congress of the United States (Washington: United States General Accounting Office).

Coomber, R. (1986) Personal communication from member of staff of Department of Health and Social Security.

Cutting, P. (1984) 'Controlled Deliveries', in Office of the Central Drugs Intelligence Unit (1984) *Confidential Intelligence Bulletin*, 7, 2, p. 20.

Davies, M. (1984) 'The Illicit Supply of and Demand for Opiates: the 10% Phenomenon', in Office of the Central Drugs Intelligence Unit (1984) *Confidential Intelligence Bulletin*, 7, 2, p. 15.

DAWN (1984) *Women and Heroin and other Opiates* (London: Drugs Alcohol Women Nationally) p. 4.

DAWN (1985) with assistance from Ettorre, E., *A Survey of Facilities for Women Using Drugs (including Alcohol) in London* (London: Drugs Alcohol Women Nationally).

Delphy, C. (1977) *The Main Enemy* (London: Women's Research and Resources Centre).

Delphy, C. and Leonard, D. (1986) 'Class Analysis, Gender Analysis and the Family', in Crompton, R. and Mann, M. (eds) *Gender and Stratification* (Cambridge: Polity Press).

DHSS (1982) *Press Release: £2million Initiative to Improve Services for Drug Misusers*, December (London: Department of Health and Social Security).

DHSS (1984) *Health Service Development: Services for Drug Misusers. Health Circular (84)14 and Local Authority Circular (84)12*, June (London: Department of Health and Social Security).

DHSS (1984) *Guidelines of Good Clinical Practice in the Treatment of Drug Misuse. Report of the Medical Working Group on Drug Dependence* (London: Department of Health and Social Security) and personal communication from its chairman Dr P. H. Connell.

DHSS (1985) *Prevalence and Service Provision: A Report on Surveys and Plans in English NHS Regions*, June (London: Department of Health and Social Security).

DHSS (1986) *Health Service Development Services for Drug Misusers. Health Circular (86) 3 and Local Authority Circular (86) 5*, February (London: Department of Health and Social Security).

Department of Health and Social Security, Department of Education and Science, Home Office, Manpower Services Commission (1985) *Government Response to the Fourth Report from the Social Services Committee 1984–5*, Cmnd 9685 (London: HMSO).

Ditton, J. and Speirits, K. (1981) *The Rapid Increase of Heroin Addiction in Glasgow during 1981* (Glasgow: University of Glasgow).

Donzelot, J. (1980) *The Policing of Families* (London: Hutchinson).

Dorn, N. (1986) 'Media Campaigns', *Druglink*, 1, 2, July/August, pp. 8–9.

Dorn, N., James, C. and South, N. (1987) *The Limits of Informal Surveillance: Four Case Studies in Identifying Neighbourhood Heroin Problems* (London: ISDD).

Dorn, N., Ribbens, J. and South, N. (1987) *Coping with a Nightmare: Family Feelings about Long Term Drug Use* (London: ISDD).

Dorn, N. and South, N. (1985) *Helping Drug Users* (Aldershot: Gower).

Edwards, G. (1969) 'The British Approach to the Treatment of Heroin Addiction', *Lancet*, 12 April, pp. 768–72.

Ettorre, B. (1987) 'Drug Problems and the Voluntary Sector of Care in the UK: Identifying Key Issues', *British Journal of Addiction*, 82, 5, pp. 469–76.

Expert Committee on Mental Health (1967) *Fourteenth Report* (Geneva: World Health Organisation).

Feldman, H. (1968) 'Ideological Supports to Becoming and Remaining a Heroin Addict', *Journal of Health and Social Behaviour*, 9, 2, pp. 131–9.

Ferman, L. and Ferman, P. (1973) 'The Structural Underpinnings of the Irregular Economy', *Poverty and Human Resources Abstracts*, 8, March, pp. 3–17.

Finch, J. and Groves, D. (eds) (1983) *A Labour of Love: Women, Work and Caring* (London: Routledge & Kegan Paul).

Finestone, H. (1957) 'Cats, Kicks and Colour', *Social Problems*, 5, p. 1.

Firestone, S. (1979) *The Dialectic of Sex* (London: The Women's Press) and (1971) (London: Jonathan Cape).

Foucault, M. (1980) *Power/Knowledge: Selected Interviews and Other Writings 1972–1977 by Michel Foucault*, ed. Colin Gordon (Brighton: Harvester Press).

Fox, A. (1979) *Yorkshire Report* (London: Hungerford Project, mimeo).

Gandossy, R., Cohen, J., Harwood, H. and Williams, J. (1980) *Drugs and Crime: A Survey and Analysis of the Literature* (Washington, US Department of Justice).

Ghodse, H. (1977) 'Casualty Departments and the Monitoring of Drug Dependence', *British Medical Journal*, 1, pp. 381–2.

Ghodse, H. (1979) 'Recommendations by Accident and Emergency Staff about Drug-overdose Patients', *Social Science and Medicine*, 13A, pp. 169–73.

Ghodse, H. *et al.* (1981) 'Drug-related Problems in London Accident and Emergency Departments: A Twelve-month Survey', *The Lancet*, 17, October.

Gill, O. (1977) *Luke Street* (London: Macmillan).

Glanz, A. (1986) 'Findings of a National Survey of the Role of General Practitioners in the Treatment of Opiate Misuse: Dealing with the Opiate Misuser', *British Medical Journal*, 293, 6545, August, 23, pp. 486–8.

Glanz, A. and Taylor, C. (1986) 'Findings of a National Survey of the Role of General Practitioners in the Treatment of Opiate Misuse: Extent of Contact with Opiate Misusers', *British Medical Journal*, 293, 6544, August, 16, pp. 427–30.

Godfrey, N. (1984) 'Waging War on the Smugglers', *Police Review*, 92, 4768, pp. 1308–9.

Goodsir, J. (1986) 'Drug Trafficking Offences Bill Could Backfire', *Druglink*, 1, 1, May/June, p. 5.

Graham, H. (1976) 'Smoking in Pregnancy: The Attitude of Expectant Mothers', *Social Science and Medicine*, 10, pp. 399–405.

Graham, H. (1983) 'Caring: A Labour of Love', in Finch and Groves (1983).

Graham, H. (1984) *Women, Health and the Family* (Brighton: Harvester Press).

Greenberg, S. and Adler, F. (1974) 'Crime and Addiction: An Empirical Analysis of the Literature, 1920–1973', *Contemporary Drug Problems*, 3, 2, pp. 2211–70.

Griffin, C. (1985) 'Turning the Tables: Feminist Analysis of Youth Unemployment', *Youth and Policy*, p. 14.

Guardian (1986a) 'Cocaine seige', January; (1986b) 'Drug trafficking crackdown fails, Fowler admits', 19 March; (1986c) 'Let drug profits go to help victims call', 22 January; (1986d) 'Banks check accounts for drug profits', 10 October.

Hakim, C. (1982) 'The social consequences of high unemployment', *Journal of Social Policy*, 11, p. 4.

Hall, S., Critcher, C., Jefferson, T., Clarke, J. and Roberts, B. (1978) *Policing the Crisis: Mugging, the State and Law and Order* (London: Macmillan).

Hansard (1985) 'Drug Trafficking', 1365, col. 771.

Hartnoll, R. (1984) 'An Overview of Heroin and Other Drugs in Britain', paper presented to the Conference on Heroin Trafficking of the Customs and Excise Group of the Society of Civil and Public Servants, London.

Hartnoll, R., Mitcheson, M., Battersby, A., Brown, G., Ellis, M., Fleming, P. and Hedley, N. (1980) 'Evaluation of Heroin Maintenance in Controlled Trial', *Archives of General Psychiatry*, 37, pp. 877–84.

Hartnoll, R., Lewis, R., Mitcheson, M. and Bryer, S. (1985) 'Estimating the Prevalence of Opioid Dependence', *Lancet*, 1, 8422; pp. 203–5.

Helmer, J. (1975) *Drugs and Minority Oppression* (New York: Seabury Press).

Henman, A., Lewis, R. and Malyon, T. (eds) (1985) *Big Deal: The Politics of the Illicit Drugs Business* (London: Pluto Press).

Henman, A. (1985) 'Cocaine Futures', in Henman *et al.* (1985).

Home Affairs Committee (1986) First Report, *Misuse of Hard Drugs*, Session 1985/6 (UK: House of Commons).

Home Affairs Select Committee (1986) *First Report of Home Affairs Committee: Misuse of Hard Drugs* (paper 66) (London: HMSO).

Home Office (1984) *Statistics of the Misuse of Drugs in the United Kingdom, 1983*, Home Office Statistical Bulletin, 18, p. 84.

Home Office (1985) *Statistics of the Misuse of Drugs in the United Kingdom, 1984*, Home Office Statistical Bulletin, 23, p. 85.

Home Office (1985) *Tackling Drug Misuse: A Summary of the Government's Strategy* (London: HMSO) 1st edn.

Home Office (1986) *Tackling Drug Misuse: A Summary of the Government's Strategy* (London: HMSO) 2nd edn.

Home Office (1986) *Statistics of the Misuse of Drugs in the United Kingdom, 1985*, Home Office Statistical Bulletin.

Hough, M. and Mayhew, P. (1983) *The British Crime Survey*, Home Office Research Study, 1976 (London: HMSO).

Hughes, P. (1977) *Behind the Wall of Respect: Community Experiments in Heroin Addiction Control* (Chicago: University of Chicago Press).

Hughes, P., Crawford, G., Barker, N., Schumann, S. and Jaffe, J. (1971) 'The Social Structure of a Heroin-copping Community', *American Journal of Psychiatry*, 128, p. 5.

Hughes, P., Barker, N., Crawford, G. and Jaffe, J. (1972) 'The Natural History of a Heroin Epidemic', *American Journal of Public Health*, 62, p. 7.

Hughes, P. and Crawford, G. (1972) 'A Contagious Disease Model for Researching and Intervening in Heroin Epidemics', *Archives of General Psychiatry*, 27, 2, pp. 149–155.

ISDD (1984) *Surveys and Statistics on Drug-taking in Britain* (London: Institute for the Study of Drug Dependence).

ISDD (1986) *Official Statistics on Drug-taking in Britain* (London: Institute for the Study of Drug Dependence).

Interdepartmental Committee (Brain Committee) (1965) *Drug Addiction. The Second Report of the Interdepartmental Committee* (London: HMSO).

International Narcotics Control Board (1983) *Statistics on Narcotic Drugs for 1983* (New York: United Nations) p. xiv.

Ives, R. (1986) 'The rise and fall of the solvents panic', *Druglink*, 1, 4, November/December, pp. 10–12.

Jagger, E. (in preparation) 'The Policing of Families: a case study of solvent abuse', PhD thesis, Department of Social Policy and Social Work, Edinburgh University.

Jahoda, M. (1982) *Employment and Unemployment: A Social-Psychological Analysis* (Cambridge University Press).

Jahoda, M., Lazarsfeld, P. and Zeisel, H. (1938) *Marienthal: The Sociography of an Unemployed Community* (London: Tavistock) 1972 edn.

Jamieson, A., Glanz, A. and MacGregor, S. (1984) *Dealing with Drug Misuse: Crisis Intervention in the City* (London: Tavistock).

Johnson, B., Goldstein, P., Preble, E., Schmeidler, J., Lipton, D., Spunt, B. and Miller, T. (1985) *Taking Care of Business: The Economics of Crime by Heroin Abusers* (Lexington: Heath/Lexington Books).

Judson, H. (1973) *Heroin Addiction in Britain* (New York: Harcourt Brace Jovanovich).

Kohn, M. (1971) 'Social Class and Parent–Child Relationships', in Anderson, M. (ed.) *Sociology of the Family* (Harmondsworth: Penguin).

Labour Party (1986) *Health for All: Charter on Preventive Health* (London: Labour Party).

Lea, J. and Young, J. (1984) *What Is To Be Done About Law and Order?* (Harmondsworth: Penguin).

Leamy, W. (1983) 'Interpol', in Office of the Central Drugs Intelligence Unit (1984) *Confidential Intelligence Bulletin*, 7, 2, p. 8.

Lewis, R. (1985) 'Serious Business – the Global Heroin Economy', in Henman *et al.* (1985).

Lewis, R., Hartnoll, R., Bryer, S., Daviaud, E. and Mitcheson, M. (1985) 'Scoring Smack: The Illicit Heroin Market in London, 1980–83', *British Journal of Addiction*. 80, 3, pp. 281–290.

Linblad, R. (1983) 'A Review of the Concerned Parents Movement in the USA', *Bulletin on Narcotics*, 25, 3, July/September, pp. 41–52.

Lindesmith, A. (1965) *The Addict and the Law* (London: Indiana University Press).

MacGregor, S. (1986) *Services for Drug Misusers*, paper commissioned for ESRC Consultative Committee (London: Economic and Social Research Council).

MacInness, C. (1985) *City of Spades* (London: Alison & Busby).

Maden, T. and Wallace, M. (1986) 'Is Saying No Enough?', *The Maudsley and Bethlem Gazette*, 311, p. 4.

Malyon, T. (1985) 'Love Seeds and Cash Crops – the Cannabis Commodity Market', in Henman *et al.* (1985).

Maxfield, M. (1984) *Fear of Crime in England and Wales*, Home Office Research Study, 78 (London: HMSO).

McCoy, A., Read, C. and Adams, L. (1972) *The Politics of Heroin in South-East Asia* (New York: Harper & Row).

Medical Working Group on Drug Dependence (1984) *Guidelines of Good Clinical Practice in the Treatment of Drug Misuse* (London: Department of Health and Social Security).

Mellor, D. Junior Home Office Minister (1986) 'Minutes of Evidence', 27 March 1985, Examination of Witnesses', in House of Commons Home Affairs Committee, *First Report from the Home Affairs Committee: Session 1985–86: Misuse of Hard Drugs* (London: HMSO).

Merton, R. (1938) 'Social Structure and Anomie', *American Sociological Review*, 3.

Merton, R. (1957) *Social Theory and Social Structure* (New York: Free Press).

Meyer, A. (1952) *Social and Psychological Factors in Opiate Addiction: A Review of Research Findings together with an Annotated Bibliography* (New York: Columbia University) pp. 87–8.

Mills, C. Wright (1970) *The Sociological Imagination* (Harmondsworth: Penguin).

Ministry of Health (1926) *Report of the Departmental Committee on Morphine and Heroine Addiction*, Rolleston Committee (London: Ministry of Health).

Ministry of Health (1967a) *Treatment and Supervision of Heroin Addiction*, HM (67) 16 (London: HMSO).

Ministry of Health (1967b) *The Rehabilitation and After Care of Heroin Addicts*, HM (67) 83 (London: HMSO).

Moore, M. (1977) *Buy and Bust: The Effective Regulation of an Illicit Market in Heroin* (Lexington: D.C. Heath/Lexington Books).

Morris, T. and Morris, P. (1955) 'Social Casework and the Healthy Community', *Case Conference*, 1.

Mott, J. (1981) 'Criminal Involvement and Penal Responses', in Edwards, G. and Busch, C. (eds) *Drug Problems in Britain* (London: Academic Press) pp. 218–43.

NACRO (1975) *Housing Management and the Prevention of Crime*, Report of a Conference, March, National Association for Care and Resettlement of Offenders.

Narcotics Control Digest (news story) (1986) 'House passes $17billion drug Bill which is likely to go for Reagan's signature; compromise with Senate over controversial death penalty issue', *Narcotics Control Digest*, 16, 21, 17 October (Washington: Washington News Crime Services) pp. 1–10.

NIDA (1965) *Epidemiology of Drug Abuse: Clinical and Social Perspectives*, Community Epidemiology Work Group Proceedings (Rockville: National Institute on Drug Abuse).

O'Bryan, L. (1985a) *Adolescent Research Project: Interim Report to the DHSS* (London: Birkbeck College, Drug Indicators Project).

O'Bryan, L. (1985b) 'The Cost of Lacoste: Drugs, Style and Money', in Henman *et al.* (1985).

Observer (1986) 'Drug Daily' 31 August.

Office of Central Drugs Intelligence Unit (1984) *Confidential Intelligence Bulletin*, 7, p. 20.

Office of Health Economics (1967) *Drug Addiction* (London: Office of Health Economics).

O'Neill, P. *et al.* (1984) 'Illicitly Imported Heroin Products: Some Physical and Chemical Features Indicative of their Origin', *Journal of Forensic Sciences*, 29, 3, pp. 889–902.

Owen, D. (1985) 'The Drugs Problem: People and Policies', Prime's Second Annual Lecture, St Thomas's Hospital, 15 October (mimeo).

PNCB (1986) *Report on National Survey of Drug Abuse* (Islamabad: Pakistan Narcotics Control Board).

Parker, H., Bakx, K. and Newcombe, R. (1986) *Drug Misuse in Wirral: A Study of Eighteen Hundred Problem Drug Users* (Liverpool: University of Liverpool).

Parkes, D. and Wallis, W. (1978) 'Graph Theory and the Study of Activity Structures', in Caristein, T., Parkes, D. and Thrift, N. (eds) *Human Activity and Time Geography* (London: Edward Arnold).

Parsons, T. (1954) *Essays in Sociological Theory* (Chicago: Free Press).

Pattison, C., Barnes, E. and Thorley, A. (1982) *South Tyneside Drug Prevalence and Indicators Study* (Newcastle-upon-Tyne: Centre for Alcohol and Drug Studies).

Pead, D. (1984) 'Why It's No Longer Enough to Nick Local Junkies', *Police Review*, 93, p. 1358.

Pearson, G. (1983) *Hooligan: A History of Respectable Fears* (London: Macmillan).

Pearson, G. (1986) 'Developing a Local Research Strategy', in Wedge, P. (ed.) *Social Work: Research into Practice* (London: British Association of Social Workers).

Pearson, G. (1987a) *The New Heroin Users* (London: Blackwell).

Pearson, G. (1987b) 'Short Memories: Street Violence in the Past and in the Present', in Moonman, E. (ed.) *The Violent Society* (London: Frank Cass).

Pearson, G. (1987c) 'Social Work and Unemployment', in Langan, M. and Lee, P. (eds) *Social Work in Recession* (London: Hutchinson).

Pearson, G., Gilman, M. and McIver, S. (1986) *Young People and Heroin: An Examination of Heroin Use in the North of England*, Research Report, 8 (London: Health Education Council) and (Aldershot: Gower) (1987).

Peck, D. and Plant, M. (1986) 'Unemployment and Illegal Drug Use: Concordant Evidence from a Prospective Study and from National Trends', *British Medical Journal*, 293, 11 October.

Peele, S. (1985) *The Meaning of Addiction* (Lexington: Heath/Lexington Books).

Penrose, R. (1985) 'The War We've Got To Win', *Police*, 18, p. 2.

Preble, E. and Casey, J. (1969) 'Taking Care of Business: The Heroin User's Life on the Streets', *International Journal of the Addictions*, 4, 1, pp. 1–24.

Readers Digest/AA (1985) *New Book of the Road* (London: Readers Digest/Automobile Association).

Reid, D. (1976) 'The Decline of Saint Monday, 1776–1876', *Past and Present*, 71.

Research Triangle Institute (1976) *Drug Use and Crime* (North Carolina: Research Triangle Institute) p. 54.

Reynolds, F. (1985) *The Problem Housing Estate* (Aldershot: Gower).

Rigby, J. (1985) 'Police and Customs Working to Stem the Flood', *Police*, 18, p. 2.

Rose, M. (1984) 'Mama Coca, the Medicine', *New Internationalist*, 140, October.

Rosenbaum, M. (1981) *Women on Heroin* (New Brunswick: Rutgers University Press).

Rosenbaum, M. (1985) 'A Matter of Style: Variation among Methadone Clinics in the Control of Clients', *Contemporary Drug Problems*, 12, pp. 375–99.

Rottenberg, S. (1968) 'The Clandestine Distribution of Heroin, Its Discovery and Suppression', *Journal of Political Economy*, January, pp. 78–90.

Rounsaville, B. Weissman, M. and Kleber, H. (1982) 'The Significance of Alcoholism in Treated Opiate Addicts', *Journal of Nervous and Mental Disease*, 170, 8, pp. 479–88.

RCMP (1983) *National Drugs Intelligence Estimate 1982* (Ottawa: Royal Canadian Mounted Police).

Schur, E. (1963) *Narcotic Addiction in Britain and America* (London: Tavistock).

Schur, E. (1965) *Crimes Without Victims* (Englewood Cliffs: Prentice-Hall).

Seccombe, W. (1974) 'The Housewife and Her Labour under Capitalism', *New Left Review*, 83, pp. 3–24.

Select Committee on Narcotics Abuse and Control (1977) *Summary of Testimony and Findings and Conclusions from Oversight Hearings on Narcotics Abuse and Control*, Interim report number 95–32 from first session of 95th Congress (Washington: US Government Printing Office).

Simmel, G. (1950) 'The Metropolis and Mental Life', in Wolff, K. (ed.) *The Sociology of Georg Simmel* (New York: Free Press).

Simmons, L. and Said, A. (eds) (1974) *Drugs, Politics and Diplomacy: The International Connection* (Beverly Hills: Sage).

Smart, C. (1984) 'Social Policy and Drug Addiction: A Critical Study of Policy Development', *British Journal of Addiction*, 79, pp. 31–9.

Smart, C. (1985) 'Drug Dependence Units in England and Wales: The Results of a National Survey', *Drug and Alcohol Dependence*, 15, pp. 131–44.

Social Services Committee (1985) *Fourth Report of the Social Services Committee: Misuse of Drugs: With Special Reference to the Treatment and Rehabilitation of Misusers of Hard Drugs (paper 208)* (London: HMSO).

SCPS (1985) *United Kingdom – Open House for Smugglers* (London: Society of Civil and Public Servants).

SCPS (1986) *UK – Drugs Unlimited* (London: Society of Civil and Public Servants).

Spear, H. (1969) 'The Growth of Heroin Addiction in the United Kingdom', *British Journal of Addiction*, 64, 2, pp. 245–55.

Spear, H. B. (1985) 'Drug Abuser Deaths', *British Journal of Addiction*, 78, 2, pp. 173–9.

Standing Conference on Drug Abuse (1985) *Memorandum submitted to Social Services Committee Session 1984–1985 Misuse of Drugs* (London: HMSO).

Stimmel, B. and Kreek, M. (1975) 'Pharmacological Actions of Heroin', in Stimmel, B. (ed.) *Heroin Dependency: Medical, Economic and Social Aspects* (New York: Stratten) pp. 71–87.

Stimson, G. (1984) 'Making Sense of Official Statistics', *British Journal of Addiction*, 79, p. 373.

Stimson, G. (1987) 'British Drug Policies in the 1980s: A Preliminary Analysis and Suggestions for Research' (forthcoming) in *British Journal of Addiction*.

Stimson, G. and Oppenheimer, E. (1982) *Heroin Addiction: Treatment and Control in Britain* (London: Tavistock).

Strang, J. (1984) 'Changing the Image of the Drug-taker', *Health and Social Services Journal*, 11 October.

Strang, J. (1985) 'Treatment of Drug Dependence – the Role of the Satellite Clinic', *Health Trends*, 17, p. 1.

Sutter, A. (1966) 'The World of the Righteous Dope-fiend', *Issues in Criminology*, 2, p. 2.

Tauqueer Sheikh, A. (1986) 'Afghanistan: Washington's Role', *The Muslim* (Islamabad) 3 November, p. 4.

Taylor, I. (1981) *Law and Order: Arguments for Socialism* (London: Macmillan).

Thompson, E. P. (1967) 'Time, Work Discipline and Industrial Capitalism', *Past and Present*, 38.

Times, The, Wednesday, 13 August, 1980, p. 13.

Trebach, A. (1982) *The Heroin Solution* (New Haven: Yale University Press).

UN Commission on Narcotic Drugs (1985) *Situation and Trends in Drug Abuse and the Illicit Traffic, including Reports of Subsidiary Bodies Concerned with the Illicit Traffic in Drugs; Review of the Illicit Traffic* (New York: United Nations).

US General Accounting Office (1985) *Coordination of Federal Drug Interdiction Efforts*, report to House of Representatives (Washington: United States General Accounting Office).

Wardlaw, G. (1978) *Drug-use and Crime: An Examination of Drug Users and Associated Persons and Their Influence on Crime Patterns in Australia* (Canberra: Australian Institute of Criminology) p. 89.

Weil, A. and Rosen, W. (1983) *Chocolate to Morphine: Understanding Mind-active Drugs* (Boston: Houghton Mifflin).

Working Party on Drug Abuse in Southwark (1985) *Report to Working Conference*, 14 April (London: Southwark).

Yates, R. (1982) *Recreation or Desperation: A Practical Guide to Assessing Drug Problems* (Manchester: Lifeline Project).

Young, J. (1973) 'The Myth of the Drug-taker in the Mass Media', in Cohen, S. and Young, J. (eds) *The Manufacture of News: Deviance, Social Problems and the Mass Media* (London: Constable).

Zawadski, B. and Lazarsfeld, P. (1935) 'The Psychological Consequences of Unemployment', *Journal of Social Psychology*, 6, pp. 224–51.

Zinberg, N. (1984) *Drug, Set and Setting: The Basis for Controlled Intoxicant Use* (New Haven: Yale University Press).

Author index

Subject index